impact
1B

SERIES EDITORS
JoAnn (Jodi) Crandall
Joan Kang Shin

STUDENT'S BOOK AUTHOR
Lesley Koustaff

Australia • Brazil • Mexico • Singapore • United Kingdom • United States

Thank you to the educators who provided invaluable feedback during the development of *Impact*:

EXPERT PANEL

Márcia Ferreira, Academic Coordinator, CCBEU, Franca, Brazil

Jianwei Song, Vice-general Manager, Ensure International Education, Harbin, China

María Eugenia Flores, Academic Director, and **Liana Rojas-Binda**, Head of Recruitment & Training, Centro Cultural Costarricense-Norteamericano, San José, Costa Rica

Liani Setiawati, M.Pd., SMPK 1 BPK PENABUR Bandung, Bandung, Indonesia

Micaela Fernandes, Head of Research and Development Committee and Assessment Committee, Pui Ching Middle School, Macau

Héctor Sánchez Lozano, Academic Director, and **Carolina Tripodi**, Head of the Juniors Program, Proulex, Guadalajara, Mexico

Rosario Giraldez, Academic Director, Alianza Cultural, Montevideo, Uruguay

REVIEWERS

BRAZIL
Renata Cardoso, Colégio do Sol, Guara, DF

Fábio Delano Vidal Carneiro, Colégio Sete de Setembro, Fortaleza

Cristiano Carvalho, Centro Educacional Leonardo da Vinci, Vitória

Silvia Corrêa, Associação Alumni, São Paulo

Carol Espinosa, Associação Cultural Brasil Estados Unidos, Salvador

Marcia Ferreira, Centro Cultural Brasil Estados Unidos, Franca

Clara Haddad, ELT Consultant, São Paulo

Elaine Carvalho Chaves Hodgson, Colégio Militar de Brasília, Brasília

Thays Farias Galvão Ladosky, Associação Brasil América, Recife

Itana Lins, Colégio Anchieta, Salvador

Samantha Mascarenhas, Associação Cultural Brasil Estados Unidos, Salvador

Ann Marie Moreira, Pan American School of Bahia, Bahia

Rodrigo Ramirez, CEETEPS- Fatec Zona Sul, São Paulo

Paulo Torres, Vitória Municipality, Vitória

Renata Zainotte, Go Up Idiomas, Rio de Janeiro

CHINA
Zhou Chao, MaxEn Education, Beijing

Zhu Haojun, Only International Education, Shanghai

Su Jing, Beijing Chengxun International English School, Beijing

Jianjun Shen, Phoenix City International School, Guangzhou

COSTA RICA
Luis Antonio Quesada-Umaña, Centro Cultural Costarricense Norteamericano, San José

INDONESIA
Luz S. Ismail, M.A., LIA Institute of Language and Vocational Training, Jakarta

Selestin Zainuddin, LIA Institute of Language and Vocational Training, Jakarta

Rosalia Dian Devitasari, SMP Kolese Kanisius, Jakarta

JAPAN
John Williams, Tezukayama Gakuen, Nara

MEXICO
Nefertiti González, Instituto Mexicano Madero, Puebla

Eugenia Islas, Instituto Tlalpan, Mexico City

Marta MM Seguí, Colegio Velmont A.C., Puebla

SOUTH KOREA
Min Yuol (Alvin) Cho, Global Leader English Education, Yong In

THAILAND
Panitnan Kalayanapong, Eduzone Co., Ltd., Bangkok

TURKEY
Damla Çaltuğ, İELEV, Istanbul

Basak Nalcakar Demiralp, Ankara Sinav College, Ankara

Humeyra Olcayli, İstanbul Bilim College, Istanbul

VIETNAM
Chantal Kruger, ILA Vietnam, Hô Chí Minh

Ai Nguyen Huynh, Vietnam USA Society, Hô Chí Minh

impact
1B

	Scope and Sequence	4
	Meet the Explorers	5

STUDENT'S BOOK:

Unit 5	What We Wear	76
Unit 6	Mix and Mash	92
	Express Yourself: Feature article	108
Unit 7	Cool Apps and Gadgets	110
Unit 8	Into the Past	126
	Express Yourself: Letter for a time capsule	142
	Pronunciation	144
	Irregular Verbs	148
	Social and Academic Language	149
	Cutouts	163

WORKBOOK:

Unit 5	What We Wear	46
Unit 6	Mix and Mash	56
	Units 5-6 Review	66
Unit 7	Cool Apps and Gadgets	68
Unit 8	Into the Past	78
	Units 7-8 Review	88
	Choice Activities	94

Scope and Sequence

5 What We Wear
page 76

6 Mix and Mash
page 92

7 Cool Apps and Gadgets
page 110

8 Into the Past
page 126

	5	6	7	8
THEME	Clothing and accessories throughout history	Mash-ups	Useful and interesting technology	Exploring the distant past
VOCABULARY STRATEGIES	· Prefix *re-* · Use a dictionary: Pronunciation	· Multiple-meaning words · Use context: Examples	· Suffix *-ible* · Identify parts of speech	· Suffix *-ful* · Context clues: Definitions and examples
SPEAKING STRATEGY	Asking for opinions; Agreeing and disagreeing	Clarifying a point	Making and responding to requests	Talking about likes and dislikes
GRAMMAR	**Past simple:** Saying what happened *Ancient Greek women preferred golden hair to dark hair.* **Past simple:** Saying what happened *Doctors wore special protective suits.*	**Adjectives:** Comparing two or more things *Underwater hockey is more difficult than field hockey.* **Countable and uncountable nouns:** Talking about amounts *Some meals are a mix of food from different cultures.*	**Superlatives:** Talking about extremes *The newest version of this game is going to be amazing.* ***Will*** **and** ***going to:*** Talking about the future *People won't talk to each other on smartphones anymore.*	**Present perfect:** Describing a past action that still continues *Games have always been a popular activity.* **There + to be:** Expressing existence at different points in time *There have always been sun celebrations around the world.*
READING	*Jewellery Talks*	*A Feast for the Eyes*	*Thinking Outside the Box*	*Growing Up: Then and Now*
READING STRATEGY	Make a personal connection	Visualise	Identify main idea and details	Identify cause and effect
VIDEO	*What to Wear*	*What's in a Mash-Up?*	*From Gadgets to Apps*	*A Journey Back in Time*
WRITING	Genre: **Descriptive paragraph** Focus: Publish	Genre: **Paragraph of exemplification** Focus: Introduce examples	Genre: **Product review** Focus: Use examples and adjectives	Genre: **Classification paragraph** Focus: Write a concluding sentence
MISSION	**Learn to Adapt** National Geographic Explorer: **Andrés Ruzo**, Geoscientist	**Be Unique** National Geographic Explorer: **Josh Ponte**, Musical Explorer/Filmmaker	**Always Keep Learning** National Geographic Explorer: **Manu Prakash**, Biophysicist	**Understand the Past** National Geographic Explorer: **Alberto Nava Blank**, Underwater Cave Explorer/Cartographer
PRONUNCIATION	The *-ed* ending	Linking: Consonant + vowel sounds	The two-vowel rule	The schwa (/ə/) sound
EXPRESS YOURSELF	Creative Expression: **Feature article** *Get Steampunked* Making connections: Fashion mash-ups		Creative Expression: **Letter for a time capsule** *Transport of Tomorrow* Making connections: Past, present and future technology	

4

Meet the Explorers

Unit 5
ANDRÉS RUZO Geoscientist

Andrés Ruzo grew up between Nicaragua, Peru and Texas. As a boy in Lima, Peru, he heard a legend about a boiling river. He is now the first geoscientist given permission to study that boiling river. His work can be dangerous. A local shaman told him, 'Use your feet like eyes.' You can't see heat, but you can feel it when you step near it. So Andrés wore sandals!

Unit 6
JOSH PONTE Musical Explorer/Filmmaker

Josh Ponte mixes traditional music with new music inspired by his travels to Gabon. Josh is helping to preserve the traditional music and dance of Gabon, much of which is disappearing. By mixing traditional music with new music, Josh is helping new generations to keep their traditions alive.

Unit 7
MANU PRAKASH Biophysicist

As a child, Manu Prakash enjoyed experimenting in an empty chemistry lab. Now he's a biophysicist who has his own lab at Stanford University. Manu believes everyone should be able to understand science. That's why he created the Foldscope, a paper microscope. He hopes that this inexpensive tool will allow more people, especially young people, to make discoveries.

Unit 8
ALBERTO NAVA BLANK Underwater Cave Explorer/Cartographer

Alberto Nava Blank dives deep into the underwater caves near Tulum, Mexico, to learn about the past. In 2007, Alberto and his team discovered the 13,000 year-old skeleton of a young girl. From this discovery, researchers have been able to learn more about how our human ancestors migrated from Asia, across the Pacific and through the Americas.

5

Unit 5

What We Wear

'The right clothes can make life a lot easier and, in some cases, even save your life.'

Andrés Ruzo

A man in a protective suit, ready to explore the Darvaza Crater, Turkmenistan

TO START

1. Describe the clothes you see in the photo. Do you think these clothes are important at this place? Why or why not?

2. What do you wear to school? On special days? At weekends?

3. What did you buy the last time you went shopping for clothing and accessories? Why did you buy these things?

77

1 **What clothes do you like to wear?**
Discuss. Then listen and read. 🎧 060

At some point, you've probably looked at old photos of people and asked yourself, 'Why did they **wear** *that*? What were they *thinking*?' The people in the photo probably thought that they **looked** great! The truth is, nothing stays the same forever, especially in the world of **fashion**. What's cool today will be ugly before long. What we like to wear changes all the time.

A **century** ago, many men – from businessmen to taxi drivers – wore **suits** to work. Even young boys regularly wore suits and **ties**. Women didn't just wear skirts or dresses when they wanted to **dress up**. They wore them all the time – even if they were just staying at home!

Over time, **casual** clothes replaced **formal** clothes. For example, **jeans** are very popular today. They were first made for workers who needed trousers with strong fabric that didn't tear easily. In 1873, tailor Jacob Davis and businessman Levi Strauss created denim trousers they called *overalls* because people wore them over their clothes. Cowboys wore denim jeans and, thanks to the Western films of the 1930s, many people began wearing them. Today, jeans and a **sweatshirt** are practically a **uniform** for teens around the world.

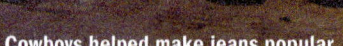
Cowboys helped make jeans popular.

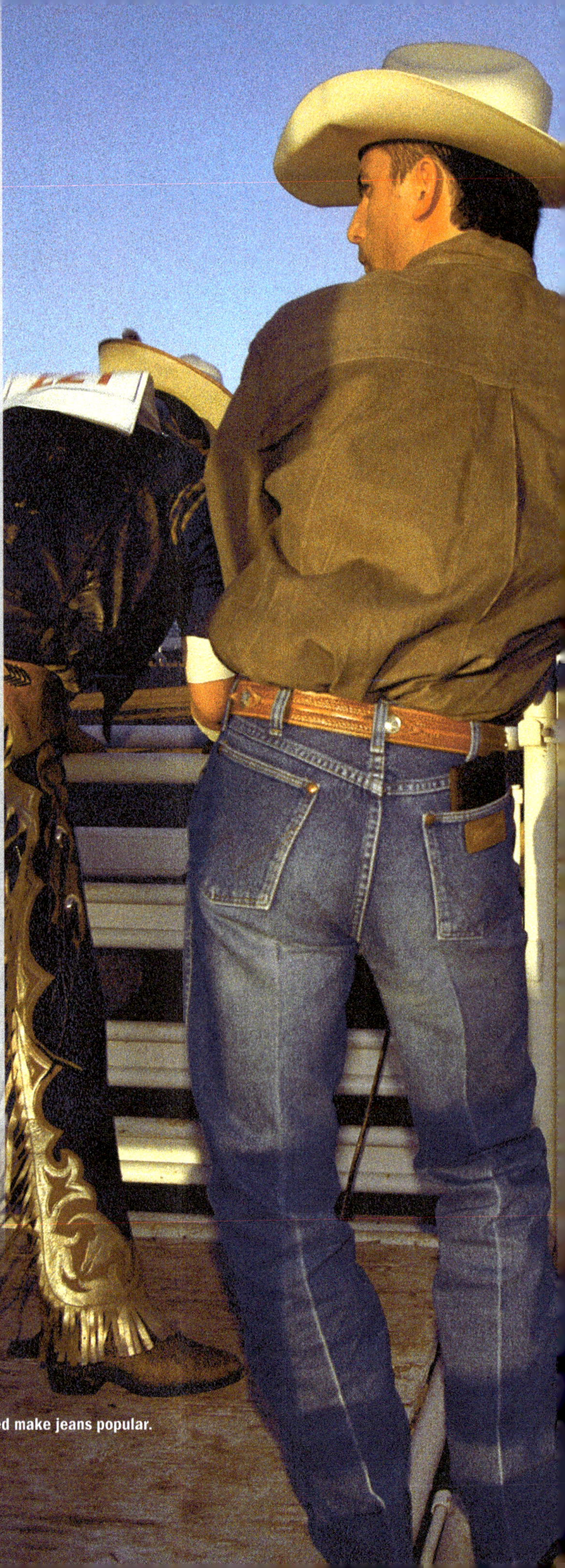

Louis XIV of France

Like clothes, shoes have also changed over time. You may prefer to wear trainers, but in the past both men and women wore shoes with high **heels**. In the early 18th century, King Louis XIV of France started wearing tights with red high-heeled shoes. This was the fashion for nearly a century before men began wearing more **practical** shoes without heels.

Things change. You might think your clothes are fashionable now, but if a hundred years from now people see a photo of you, they might just ask, 'Why did they wear *that*?'

2 **LEARN NEW WORDS** Listen and repeat. 🎧 061

3 **Work in pairs.** Think about photos that you've seen of people from long ago. Compare their clothes with what you wear now.

VOCABULARY 79

4 **Read and write the words from the list.** Make any necessary changes.

| dress up | fashion | formal | jeans | look |
| practical | suit | sweatshirt | uniform | wear |

Andrés Ruzo works with geothermal energy, which is produced using heat from the Earth. To do this, Andrés needs to work in very hot places. He _____ clothing for protection, not _____ . He can't always work in _____ and a T-shirt. Andrés doesn't wear a _____ like a police officer or a pilot does, but he does wear different clothes for different tasks. He needs to wear a special all-in-one _____ to protect himself in extremely hot, dangerous places. He also wears heavy boots to protect his feet. It might not _____ fashionable, but for Andrés, safety is more important.

Sometimes lighter clothes are safer and more _____ . On one research trip, Andrés wore shorts and sandals. The water was very hot, and he needed to quickly check the temperature. Sandals were safer than boots because boots can fill with hot water and burn his feet.

5 **LEARN NEW WORDS Listen to these words.** Use them to complete the sentences. Then listen and repeat. 🎧 062 063

| denim | fabric | replace | tights |

1. Clothes are made of _____ .

2. Girls often wear _____ with a skirt.

3. New fashion can _____ old fashion.

4. Jeans are made of _____ .

Andrés Ruzo testing hot water

6 **YOU DECIDE Choose an activity.**

1. **Work independently.** Interview a parent or grandparent. Find out how clothing has changed from when he or she was young. Write a paragraph to say what you learnt.

2. **Work in pairs.** Make a T-chart with the headings *practical* and *not practical*. Then write examples of clothes you wear under each category.

3. **Work in groups.** What percentage of your clothing is chosen for practical reasons? What percentage is for fashion? Take a poll. Compare your results with another group.

VOCABULARY

SPEAKING STRATEGY 🎧 064

Asking for opinions	Agreeing and disagreeing
<u>I think school uniforms are a good idea</u>. What do you think?	I agree. I'm not really sure. I don't agree.
<u>We shouldn't have to wear uniforms</u>. Don't you agree?	Yes, I do. Not really. <u>I think uniforms are very practical</u>.

1 **Listen.** How do the speakers ask for opinions and respond? Write the phrases you hear. 🎧 065

2 **Read and complete the dialogue.**

Bo: Agus, do students in Indonesia wear school uniforms?

Agus: Yes. Most school students wear uniforms. It's a good idea. _____

Bo: _____ Actually, in China, girls and boys wear the same uniform. So no student looks different. I like this idea.

Agus: Well, _____ . Maybe students in primary and secondary schools should wear different uniforms, like they do in Indonesia. It might be good for students to show their progress. _____

Bo: _____ I think it's more important for *all* students to look the same.

School uniforms

3 **Work in pairs.** Throw a coin and move ahead (heads = 1 space; tails = 2 spaces). When you land on a space, give your opinion. Then ask your partner's opinion. Your partner will agree or disagree.

I think our clothes show who we are. What do you think?

I agree.

Go to page 163.

SPEAKING 81

GRAMMAR 066

Past simple: Saying what happened

Ancient Greek women **preferred** golden hair to dark hair.
Did Ancient Greek men **like** to wear their hair short? No, they **didn't**.
Ancient Greek women **didn't like** short hair either.
What **did** Ancient Greek women **use** to make their hair shiny?
They **used** olive oil.

like → lik**ed**
prefer → prefer**red**
brush → brush**ed**

1 **Listen.** Circle the correct forms of the verbs you hear.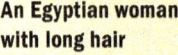

1. wanted — didn't want
2. believed — didn't believe
3. used — didn't use
4. attached — didn't attach
5. helped — didn't help
6. protected — didn't protect
7. liked — didn't like
8. washed — didn't wash
9. used — didn't use
10. mixed — didn't mix
11. coloured — didn't colour
12. loved — didn't love

An Egyptian woman with long hair

2 **Read.** Complete the sentences about women's hair in Ancient Greece. Use the correct form of the verbs in brackets.

1. How did women _____ (like) to wear their hair?

   They _____ (pull) their hair off their faces and _____ (tie) it into a knot.

2. How did they _____ (colour) their hair red?

   They _____ (comb) a special paint, called *henna*, through their hair.

3. What did they _____ (use) to curl their hair?

   They _____ (use) a metal tool, shaped like a pencil. They _____ (curl) their hair around it.

4. Did they _____ (place) anything in their hair?

   Yes, they did. They _____ (place) fresh flowers in their hair.

82 GRAMMAR

3 **LEARN NEW WORDS** **Listen to learn about how people decorate their bodies now and how they decorated them long ago.** Then listen and repeat. 068 069

People **decorate** their bodies in many ways.

Artists **paint** the hands and feet of Indian **brides** with henna.

In the past, most Maori men covered their faces in **tattoos**. Some still do today.

In some cultures, people **pierce** babies' ears to show that they're girls.

4 **Work in pairs.** Listen again. Answer the questions in complete sentences. 070

1. How did people decorate their bodies long ago?
   _____

2. What did Maori men do to their faces in the past?
   _____

3. Why did some people paint their bodies instead of getting tattoos?
   _____

4. What parts of brides' bodies did artists paint with henna?
   _____

5. What did people do to their ears 5,000 years ago that they still do today?
   _____

5 **Work in groups.** Think of people you know who have done things to change their hair and bodies. Use the past simple to describe what they did.

1 **BEFORE YOU READ** Discuss in pairs. Look at the photo. What is the woman wearing? Why do you think she's wearing it?

2 **LEARN NEW WORDS** Find these words in the dictionary. Notice how they're pronounced. Then listen and repeat. 🎧 071

| accessory | bracelet | necklace |
| outfit | wealth | |

3 **WHILE YOU READ** Think about your own habits. What type of jewellery do you wear? Why do you wear it? 🎧 072

Throughout history, people have used accessories to make their outfits look more special. Jewellery was, and still is, in fashion all over the world. Through the years, people have worn jewellery for different reasons: to make themselves look beautiful, to protect them from bad things, and to show how much money they have.

In South Africa, men in the Ndebele tribe often gave their wives jewellery made of metal rings. Ndebele women wore necklaces around their necks and bracelets around their arms. Rings were even worn on their legs. The rings showed wealth. A woman with many rings had a richer husband. In the past, women only took off the rings when their husbands died. Today, Ndebele women still wear the rings, but not all of the time.

Jewellery TALKS

HOW ACCESSORIES HELP TELL OUR STORIES

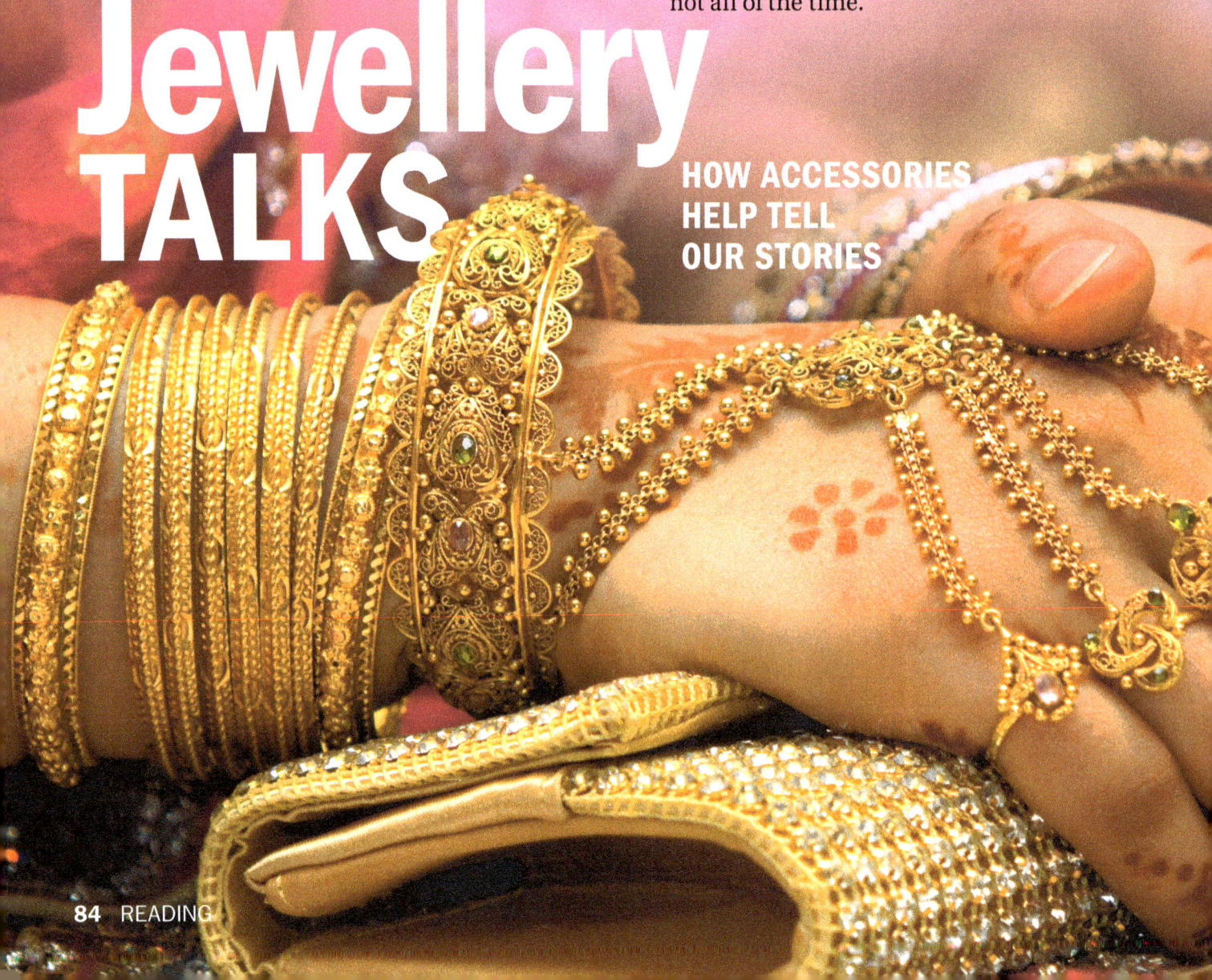

84 READING

People in India have been wearing jewellery for more than 5,000 years. In the past, both men and women wore a lot of jewellery. Women wore as many as 50 bracelets at a time! Over time, men stopped wearing so much jewellery, but for women jewellery continues to be very important. In India, jewellery means security. If a family has trouble with money, they can always sell their jewellery. And, as with the Ndebele tribe, jewellery means wealth. Indian women can expect to receive jewellery as gifts for each important life event, such as birth, marriage and becoming a mother. In addition to wearing bracelets and necklaces, Indian women might pierce their nose or wear rings on their toes.

In ancient China, people wore jewellery not just to show wealth but also for protection. They believed that the jade stone used in their jewellery was alive and that it kept bad things away. Many Chinese people today still believe this, and they wear jade bracelets for protection. They only wear the bracelets on their left arms, and they only take them off when necessary.

Jewellery is an important part of women's fashion in India.

4 AFTER YOU READ Work in pairs. Tick T for *true* or F for *false*.

1. People wear jewellery for a lot of different reasons. T F
2. Ndebele women buy their own metal rings. T F
3. Ndebele women today never take off their metal rings. T F
4. Indian women didn't wear much jewellery in the past. T F
5. Chinese people still wear jade bracelets for protection. T F
6. All jewellery today is very different from jewellery long ago. T F

5 Work in groups. Discuss your answers to Activity 3. How many answers were similar? How does your use of jewellery compare with that of the cultures you learnt about in the reading?

6 Discuss in groups.

1. Is jewellery important to you? Why or why not? Do you have a favourite piece of jewellery? If so, describe it.
2. Compare and contrast reasons why people wore jewellery long ago with reasons that people wear jewellery today. Use what you already know as well as information from the reading in your answer.
3. Imagine that you design a piece of jewellery. Who is it for? What does it say about that person? What type of jewellery is it? What does it look like?

READING 85

VIDEO ▶

① BEFORE YOU WATCH Discuss in pairs.
Imagine you're going to work in the desert for one full day. What clothes should you wear? Why? What other things should you take with you? Make a list.

② Work in pairs. In the video, you will hear about a problem the explorer Andrés Ruzo had while working in the desert. Look at the photo. What do you think the problem might be?

③ WHILE YOU WATCH Circle the words you hear. Watch scene 5.1.

boots	comfortable	cool	fashion
heels	practical	protect	shirt
shoes	suit	sweatshirt	warm

④ AFTER YOU WATCH Work in pairs to answer the questions.

1. What are the soles of boat shoes made like?
2. How are boat shoes practical?
3. What kind of environments does Andrés work in?
4. Why is the right clothing important for him?
5. What did he and his team take for protection from the sun?
6. How did the team use the item for protection?

86 VIDEO

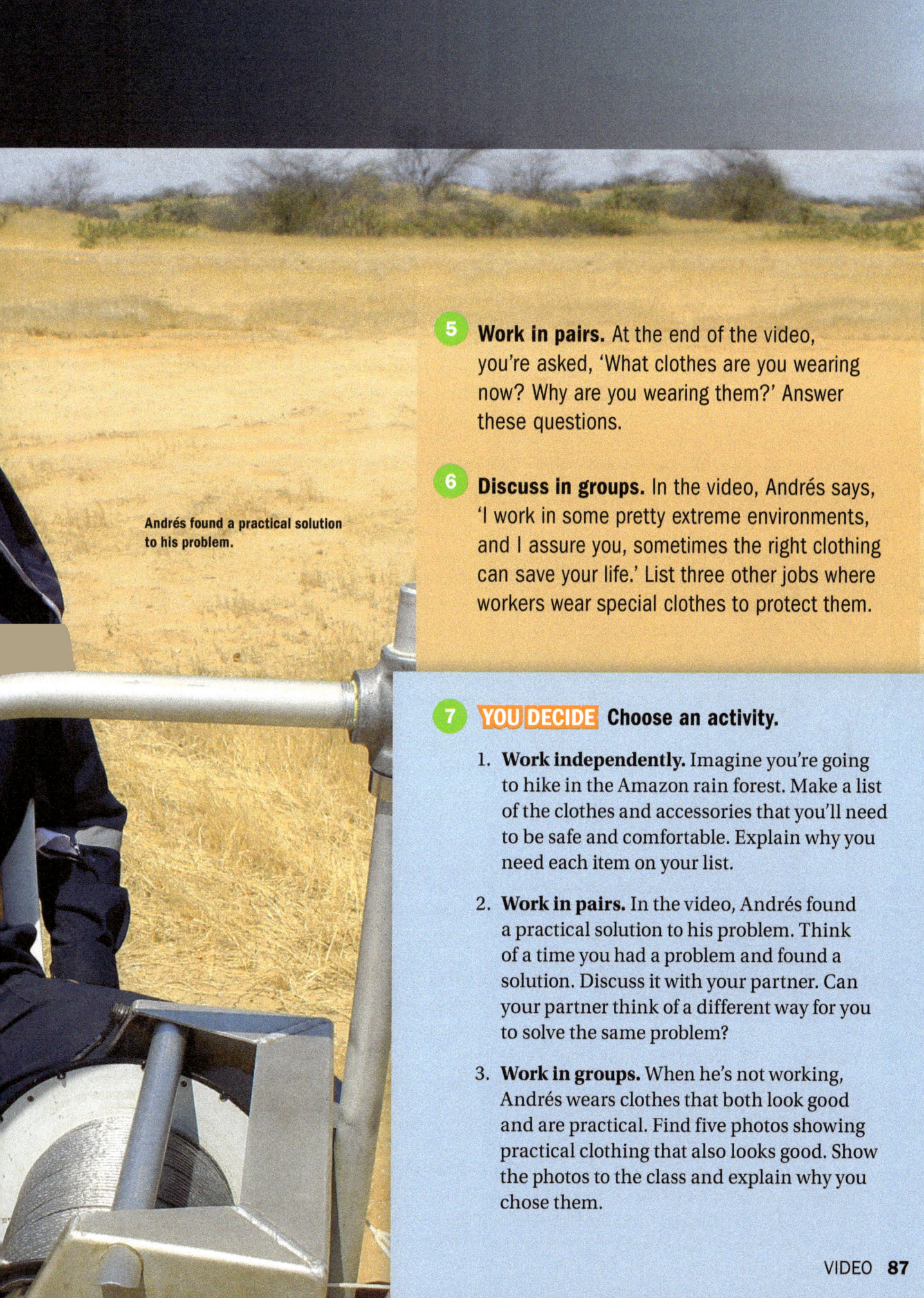

Andrés found a practical solution to his problem.

5. **Work in pairs.** At the end of the video, you're asked, 'What clothes are you wearing now? Why are you wearing them?' Answer these questions.

6. **Discuss in groups.** In the video, Andrés says, 'I work in some pretty extreme environments, and I assure you, sometimes the right clothing can save your life.' List three other jobs where workers wear special clothes to protect them.

7. **YOU DECIDE** Choose an activity.

   1. **Work independently.** Imagine you're going to hike in the Amazon rain forest. Make a list of the clothes and accessories that you'll need to be safe and comfortable. Explain why you need each item on your list.

   2. **Work in pairs.** In the video, Andrés found a practical solution to his problem. Think of a time you had a problem and found a solution. Discuss it with your partner. Can your partner think of a different way for you to solve the same problem?

   3. **Work in groups.** When he's not working, Andrés wears clothes that both look good and are practical. Find five photos showing practical clothing that also looks good. Show the photos to the class and explain why you chose them.

GRAMMAR 073

Past simple: Saying what happened

Long ago the plague **made** people very ill.

Doctors **had** to help people with the plague.

Doctors **wore** special protective suits. This way, they **didn't** get ill.

Doctors also **put** on red glasses. They **thought** the colour red would protect them.

1 **Read.** Complete the sentences with the past simple form of the verbs in brackets. For help, go to page 148.

Doctors _____ (begin) wearing protective suits in England in the mid-1300s. They _____ (think) these suits _____ (keep) them safe from a sickness called the *plague*. So they _____ (wear) birdlike masks and long leather coats. The coats _____ (go) all the way to the ground. Doctors always _____ (bring) a cane to their patients' houses. That way, they _____ (not have) to use their hands to touch the patient.

In the 1940s, people _____ (make) a new kind of protective suit. The suit _____ (not leave) any part of the body uncovered. The rubber fabric _____ (give) people good protection. People _____ (get) into the suit from the front. Then they _____ (put) on long gloves, boots and a hood. The suit _____ (have) a special machine to help them breathe.

A protective suit

2 **Work in pairs.** Throw the cube. Ask a question about the past using the words on the cube. Your partner answers the question.

What did you wear to the concert?

I wore a blue dress with black shoes.

Go to page 173.

88 GRAMMAR

WRITING

The last step in writing is publishing. After you write, review and proofread your work, you're ready to publish. When you publish, you let other people read your work.

1 Read the model. Do you think this essay is ready to be published? Why or why not? Discuss in pairs.

Before 1870, there were no football uniforms. Players wore their own clothes, which made it hard to know which team they were on. The first football uniform had long, loose shorts. Players wore striped, formal shirts with collars and buttons. The entire uniform was made of a heavy fabric, such as wool. Players then put on leather football boots that went up over their ankles.

Football uniforms have changed many times through the years. Today, football uniforms are very different. The shorts are shorter, and the whole uniform is made out of light fabric. This keeps football players cool as they run. Instead of boots, football players wear soft leather shoes. Each team now has its own colours. For example, players on the Brazilian football team wear bright yellow and green shirts, blue shorts and white socks. But these uniforms will change, too. After all, sports teams need uniforms that are practical but also in fashion!

English football players wearing uniforms, 1888

2 Discuss in pairs. Who do you think would find this essay interesting? Where should the author publish this essay?

3 Write. Research another uniform that has changed over time. Write an essay about the changes. Proofread your work. Then publish it by sharing it with your classmates.

NATIONAL GEOGRAPHIC

Learn to Adapt

'Adaptation is key to survival. Whether it's wearing a coat on a cold day or finding new sources of green energy – our ability to adapt to life's challenges allows us to thrive.'

Andrés Ruzo
National Geographic Explorer, Geoscientist

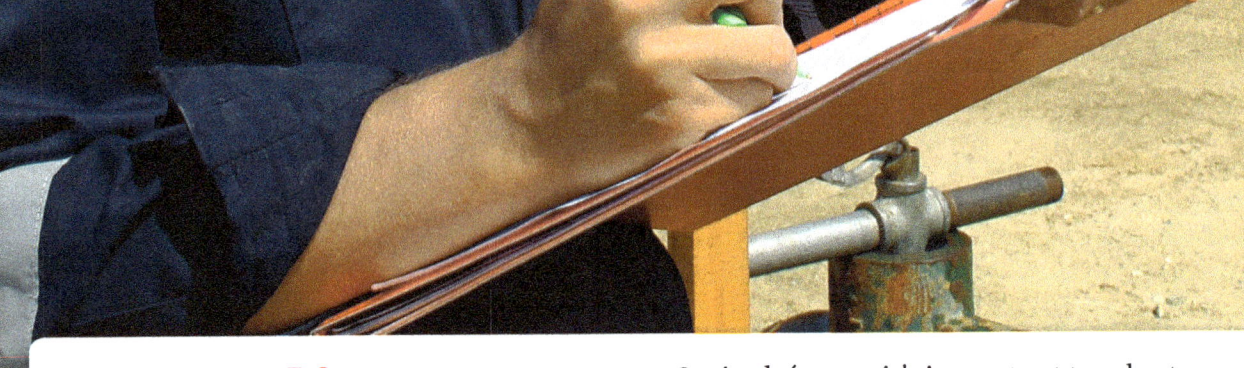

1. **Watch scene 5.2.**
2. How does the environment you're in affect your clothing choices? Give examples.
3. Andrés says it's important to adapt, or change our behaviour, to respond to what's happening around us. Give examples of a time when you did this, and a time when you didn't. What happened in each situation?

Make an Impact

YOU DECIDE Choose a project.

1 Be a clothing designer.
- Design an accessory or article of clothing that will look good and protect you.
- Draw a picture of it. Write an explanation to say why it looks good and is practical.
- Present your design to the class.

2 Plan and conduct a clothing scavenger hunt.
- As a group, prepare a list of clothing items and accessories.
- Look around your home, your school or local clothes shops. Take photos of the most interesting examples of each of the items on your list.
- Create a photo gallery to share your group's best photos. Describe the items and why you liked them.

3 Prepare a history presentation.
- Research an article of clothing or accessory not presented in this unit. Find out how it has changed over the years.
- Create a poster or computer presentation about the item you chose. Use photos to show how the item has changed.
- Share your presentation with the class.

Unit 6

Mix and Mash

'Different is OK.'
Josh Ponte

Sea is for Cookie, a mash-up created from *The Great Wave off Kanagawa* and a television character called Cookie Monster

TO START

1. What are the different parts of this image?

2. What do you think of this image?

3. Think of two things that you could put together to make something different and new. What are they? What can you make?

1 **What types of music do you like?**
Discuss. Then listen and repeat. 🎧 074

Mixing different styles of music creates a unique sound called a *mash-up*. Musicians have been creating mash-ups for more than 50 years. Many combine sounds from just two **songs**, but some might **include** parts from as many as 25 songs!

Many mash-up artists are **DJs** who use electronic equipment to mix together songs that already exist. These DJs decide what songs to use and how to mix them. Then they **record** their mash-ups. Next the DJs **edit** their **recordings** to make sure they sound as **cool** as possible.

DJs aren't the only ones that create musical mash-ups: bands do, too. One band that does this is the WagakkiBand from Japan. This band mixes the sounds of **traditional** Japanese instruments with rock music. The song they **performed** in their first **video** was a big hit. More than 30 million people saw the video on the Internet. People from all over the world downloaded the song from this video.

94 VOCABULARY

Another mash-up band is Gokh-Bi System from Dakar, Senegal. This band mixes rap with ancient West African music in a style called 'ancient-meets-urban'. The band performs with other famous singers and artists. **Fans** come from all over to hear them play.

People have different **opinions** of mash-up music. Some people prefer more traditional music styles. Others think that a mix of sounds is cooler than just one type of music. But no matter what you think of them, mash-ups provide an **audio** experience you won't forget!

2 **LEARN NEW WORDS** Listen and repeat. 075

3 **Work in pairs.** Why do you think some musicians mix modern and traditional music? Do you think it's a good idea to do this? Why or why not?

WagakkiBand with traditional and modern instruments

4 Read and write the words from the list. Make any necessary changes.

| cool | edit | fan | include | mix |
| opinion | performing | record | recording | traditional |

Filmmaker and music producer Josh Ponte travelled to communities in Gabon to _____ a film. He focused on _____ Gabonese music and dance. The journey was difficult for Josh. 'It was nuts,' he said. Josh had that _____ because on the trip he and his crew had excellent equipment, but no water and little food. In the end, Josh made more than 100 hours of _____ . These _____ music, interviews and people _____ traditional dances. Josh then _____ the videos to create a very _____ film called *Gabon: The Last Dance*. 'I hope to show where Gabon is today, in a changing world, with this astonishing music at its heart,' said Josh.

Josh Ponte filming Gabonese musicians

5 LEARN NEW WORDS Listen to these words and match them to their definitions. Then listen and repeat. 🎧 076 077

| combine | download | electronic | hit |

_____ 1. put two or more things together
_____ 2. something successful (such as a song or a film)
_____ 3. put something onto a computer
_____ 4. using electricity to produce something

6 YOU DECIDE Choose an activity.

1. **Work independently.** Interview three classmates. Find out their favourite musicians and whether any of them mix different styles of music. Report your findings to the class.

2. **Work in pairs.** Research the bands mentioned in the lesson and listen to their music. Which band's music did you like best? Which did you like least? Discuss your responses.

3. **Work in groups.** What are some traditional instruments in your country? What musical instrument from your country do you think would be good to mix with modern music? Share your ideas with the class.

96 VOCABULARY

SPEAKING STRATEGY 078

Clarifying a point

Point	Clarification
I really like fiction.	I mean, I love reading made-up stories.
I enjoy reading non-fiction books.	In other words, I like books that teach me something new.
I'm reading a book of myths.	That is, I'm reading a story that's fiction but that many people believe is true.

1 **Listen.** How do the speakers clarify their points? Write the phrases you hear. 079

A liger

2 **Read and complete the dialogue.**

Luisa: Rob, I'm reading a bizarre book. _____, it's really strange.

Rob: Really? What's it about?

Luisa: Well, the author combines a romance novel with science fiction. _____, the story mixes a love story with strange things that don't exist!

Rob: Wow! Are there monsters from outer space in the story?

Luisa: No, they're all ocean dwellers. _____, they live in the sea. Like angry sharks and evil, carnivorous jellyfish. _____, the jellyfish eat meat … and by meat, I mean people!

Rob: Is it required reading? _____, are you reading it for school?

Luisa: No, the books I read for school are never this strange!

Rob: Good! Let me borrow it when you've finished.

3 **Work in groups.** Cut out the cards and put them in a pile. Take turns choosing two cards. Make a mash-up of the two items. Draw and describe your idea. Get a point for each successful mash-up. If you can't make one, lose a turn.

I'm making a 'biscar'. In other words, I'm mixing a biscuit with a car. The car has got four giant biscuits as wheels!

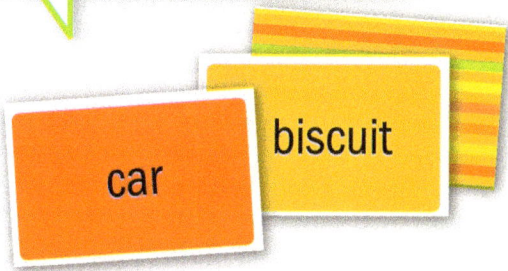

Go to page 165.

4 **Work in pairs.** Choose a book or film you both like. Then create a mash-up with another type of story. Tell your new story idea to another pair, clarifying your points.

SPEAKING 97

GRAMMAR 080

Adjectives: Comparing two or more things

Underwater hockey is a **newer** version of field hockey.
Underwater hockey is **more difficult than** field hockey.
Chess boxing is **less tiring than** boxing.
Chess boxing is **noisier than** regular chess.
The rules of boxing are **simpler / more simple than** those of chess boxing.
Ice football isn't **as popular as** traditional football.
Some fans like ice football **better than** traditional football.

hard → harder	simple → simpler
(but fun → more fun)	or more simple
noisy → noisier	difficult → more difficult

Bossaball is played on a blow-up court with trampolines.

1 **Listen.** Tick the words you hear. Then write the comparative form of each ticked word. 081

☐ fast _____   ☐ hard _____

☐ unusual _____   ☐ cool _____

☐ easy _____   ☐ enjoyable _____

☐ exciting _____   ☐ fun _____

☐ active _____   ☐ good _____

2 **Read.** Complete the sentences with the correct comparative form.

1. Kronum is _____ (+/new) bossaball, but it's _____ (=/unusual) bossaball.

2. It's _____ (+/difficult) to play than bossaball because it's a mix of football, basketball, handball and rugby.

3. The special kronum ball is _____ (+/small) a football.

4. Kronum isn't played all over the world yet, so it's _____ (–/popular) bossaball.

3 **Work in pairs.** Make a list of your five favourite sports. Then share your list with your partner. Make comparisons between those sports.

> Football is more exciting than baseball.

98 GRAMMAR

4 **LEARN NEW WORDS** **Listen and read to find out about another unusual sport.** Then listen and repeat. 🎧 082 083

Do you **hate** how expensive it is to play golf? Try disc golf instead – it's a cheaper **version** of golf. Disc golf is a **hybrid** sport. People **created** it using ideas from golf and disc-throwing. Now it's very popular. Many players **love** it!

5 **Work in pairs.** Read about the hybrid sport volcano boarding. Circle the correct words.

1. Daryn Webb *created / loved* volcano boarding because he wanted something more exciting than sandboarding.

2. Volcano boarding is a newer *version / hybrid* sport than sandboarding.

3. Volcano boarding is a more dangerous *version / hybrid* of sandboarding.

4. Some people *love / hate* volcano boarding because it's more fun and more extreme than many other hybrid sports.

5. Other people *love / hate* this sport because the ride down is noisier and less comfortable than sandboarding.

6 **Work in groups.** Compare the hybrid sports you read about (and any others you know) to traditional sports.

> Football tennis seems fun. It's a hybrid of football and tennis. It's more fun to watch than regular tennis.

GRAMMAR **99**

A Feast FOR THE Eyes

Using food to create art

We've all seen art created from paint, clay, metal and stone. But British photographer and artist Carl Warner goes to the supermarket to buy his art supplies. Carl creates what he calls *foodscapes*. He combines different types of food to imitate real landscapes. Then he photographs them. One of his foodscapes, *Carts and Balloons*, is a countryside scene. In this foodscape a few leafy green stalks of broccoli are a forest. A few pieces of bread

1 BEFORE YOU READ Discuss in pairs. Describe the most unusual piece of art you've seen. What did you like about it? What didn't you like about it?

2 LEARN NEW WORDS Find these words in the reading. What do you think they mean? Notice examples that give their meaning. Then listen and repeat. 084

| imagine | imitate | modern | original | weird |

3 WHILE YOU READ Try to visualise the artwork being described. 085

4 AFTER YOU READ Work in pairs to answer the questions.

1. What's a foodscape?
2. How did Carl create the landscape you see above?
3. Why does Carl create foodscapes?
4. Who asked Giuseppe Arcimboldo to paint his portrait?
5. Why did Giuseppe call the portrait *Vertumnus*?

Celery Island by Carl Warner

are used to make a cart. There are some berries in the cart and some potatoes as rocks. Some yellow sweetcorn and a few cucumbers are the fields. Hot-air balloons, made from bunches of bananas and other fruit, float in the sky. Some clouds of white bread float in the sky, too. It might seem a little weird to create art out of food, but Carl hopes that his work will get children excited about eating healthy foods.

Combining food and art is not a modern idea. Giuseppe Arcimboldo, a 16th-century Italian painter, also combined different types of food to create original art. In 1590, Emperor Rudolf II asked Giuseppe to paint his portrait. The result was really unusual! Called *Vertumnus*, after the Roman god of fruit, the painting shows a face made of fruit, vegetables and flowers. Giuseppe painted one pea pod for each top eyelid, two baby onions for each bottom eyelid, one grape for each eye, a pear for the nose, an apple for one cheek and a peach for the other. Can you imagine what the emperor's face looked like? Luckily, the emperor was happy with this unusual portrait!

5 Work in pairs. You read about two pieces of food art in the reading: the foodscape *Carts and Balloons* and the portrait *Vertumnus*. Choose one of the pieces to draw. Draw your pictures individually, and then compare your work. How are the pictures similar? How are they different?

6 Discuss in groups.

1. Imagine you're creating a piece of food art. What picture do you make? What foods do you use to make it?

2. What problems do you think food artists have when they work? Name two or three.

3. Imagine you're an artist. What everyday things (other than food) could you use to create art? What would you create with those things?

4. Do you think combining food and art is a good idea? Why or why not?

READING **101**

VIDEO

1 **BEFORE YOU WATCH Discuss in pairs.**

1. DJs mix music to create new songs. Why do you think they do this?
2. Choose two songs you both like. What part would you choose from each song to create your mash-up? What would your mash-up song be called?

2 **Write.** You're going to watch *What's in a Mash-Up?* Use what you've learnt in the unit so far to answer that question.

_____

_____

3 **WHILE YOU WATCH Circle the types of mash-ups mentioned in the video. Watch scene 6.1.**

| animal | art | book | fashion |
| food | music | mythical | sport |

4 **AFTER YOU WATCH Work in pairs to answer the questions.**

1. How long have people been creating mash-ups?
2. What is the Great Sphinx of Giza a mash-up of?
3. What mythical creature is a mash-up of a man and a horse?
4. What two sports combine to make up *volenis*?
5. What is another name for *food mash-up*?
6. How is a ramen burger different from a regular hamburger?

A DJ can create a mash-up by mixing music.

5. **Work in pairs.** Of all the mash-ups you've learnt about so far, which is the most interesting? The least interesting? Explain your answers.

6. **Discuss in groups.**
   1. At the end of the video, you're asked, 'What would you mash up?' Discuss your answers to this question.
   2. Give another example of a mash-up from history. Describe it and its individual parts.
   3. What do you think might be difficult in creating a mash-up? Consider art, food and music mash-ups in your answer.

7. YOU DECIDE **Choose an activity.**
   1. **Work independently.** Imagine you're a centaur. How does it help you? What's difficult about it? Write a paragraph to explain.
   2. **Work in pairs.** Think of a mash-up you know. Create an advertisement for it. Describe what it's made of and what's special about it. Present your advert to the class.
   3. **Work in groups.** In the video, you saw a historical mash-up, the Great Sphinx of Giza. Use the Internet to learn more about the Great Sphinx. Present the information to the class.

VIDEO **103**

GRAMMAR 086

Countable and uncountable nouns: Talking about amounts

Countable nouns

A few / Some / A lot of / Many meal**s are** a mix of food from different cultures.

How many chef**s combine** foods from different cultures?

Two / A few / Some / A lot of / Many chef**s combine** foods from different cultures.

Restaurants usually have **a couple of / three / too many** special dish**es**.

Uncountable nouns

A little / Some / A lot of / Much fruit **is** used in food from different cultures.

How much cheese **is** on a Japanese-Italian pizza?

A little / Some / A lot of cheese.

Dessert sushi sometimes has **a piece of / some / too much** fruit in it.

---

1 Work in pairs. Choose the correct word or phrase to complete the sentences.

Maiza: We had _____ (a few / some) delicious KoMex food last night.

Gabi: KoMex? In other words, Korean and Mexican food combined? Did they have Korean tacos?

Maiza: Yes, and _____ (much / a few) different kinds. I like beef tacos. Their tacos had _____ (a lot of / a few) Korean barbecue beef and _____ (a couple of / much) cucumber slices on fresh corn tortillas. Oh, and _____ (some / many) great sauce, too.

KoMex food

Gabi: Mmm. Sounds good. How _____ (much / many) tacos did you eat?

Maiza: Not too _____ (many / much). I only had _____ (one / a little) taco, but I had _____ (much / a lot of) nachos. They had Korean meat and mango salsa.

Gabi: Sounds great! And did you try _____ (a couple of / some) kimchi rice?

Maiza: I only ate _____ (a few / a little). I was full!

2 Work in groups. Throw the cubes. Ask and answer questions about how people in the country eat or drink the item on the cube.

How much rice do you think people in Japan eat?

I think they eat a lot of rice.

Go to page 167.

104 GRAMMAR

WRITING

When you write a paragraph of exemplification, you introduce an idea. Then you use examples to support that idea. The following phrases can help you introduce examples:

for example   one/another example is   such as

1 **Read the model.** Work in pairs to find and underline phrases that introduce examples.

Ani-mixes

Combining photos of two or more animals is a popular activity these days. There are a lot of funny and weird animal mixes that people create and share on the Internet. For example, a 'turger' is a tiger with a turtle shell. Another example is the 'dish', which is a mix of a dog and a fish. Its body has a few fins and some scales, and it has a lot of fur on its dog head. Some mixes are a little scary, such as the 'sharilla'. It's a combination of a shark and a gorilla, with the head of a shark and the body of a gorilla. It has a huge mouth with a lot of teeth in it. It has a huge, furry body, and its head and fur are almost the same colour. It's funny to look at, but I think I'd run if I saw a 'sharilla' in real life!

A 'sharilla'

2 **Discuss in pairs.** What are the three animal mixes you read about? How would you react to seeing each of them?

3 **Write.** Create your own unique ani-mix. Name it and write a paragraph about it. Give examples of what makes it unique. If possible, create a photo and include it with your paragraph.

Be Unique

'Look where everyone is looking, then turn 180 degrees and walk. You'll often find that's where the gems are.'

Josh Ponte
National Geographic Explorer, Musical Explorer/Filmmaker

1. **Watch scene 6.2.**
2. When people learnt that Josh planned to quit his job and work in Gabon, many of them thought he was taking a big risk. Do you agree? Why or why not?
3. Think of a time when you did something really different from what everyone else was doing. What did you do? Was it easy or difficult? Were you glad you did it? Why or why not?

Make an Impact

YOU DECIDE Choose a project.

1 Make and explain food art.

- Decide what to create and what food to use.
- Photograph each step as you create your art.
- Share your photographs with the class. Explain how you made your artwork.

2 Create a mash-up comic strip.

- Choose any two types of stories to mix for your mash-up. For example, mix a fairy tale and science fiction.
- Write the story in six to eight panels. Draw pictures in each panel.
- Share your story with the class.

3 Invent a hybrid sport.

- Choose two or three sports you like. Think of how to combine them.
- Write rules for your sport.
- Explain your sport. If possible, demonstrate it for the class.

Express Yourself

1 Read and listen to how to create a steampunk outfit.
🎧 087

Steampunk

Steampunk combines the fashion of Victorian England (1837–1901) with science fiction. The *steam* in steampunk refers to steam-powered machinery from the 19th century. *Punk* means breaking traditional rules.

2 Discuss in groups.

1. Do you like the steampunk look? What do you think is interesting about it? What don't you like? Explain.

2. Where do you get ideas about fashion?

Get steampunked. Here's how:

Plan Think about the character you want. Do you want to be a pilot? Or maybe a sailor? How about a scientist or a soldier? Choosing a character will help you select the best clothing and accessories.

Create Now think about what you'll wear: old-fashioned trousers and a jacket, or maybe a beautiful dress. Be creative! Make changes you want, to create something unique. For example, Victorian-era women wore high-heeled boots, but you might prefer flat shoes. Your clothing can be in any colour, though many fans of steampunk prefer dark colours.

Steampunk it! Now for the important part – accessories! If you have an outfit that looks Victorian but doesn't have accessories, it's not steampunk! Steampunk accessories can include goggles, machine parts, old watches, leather belts or interesting hats. Remember to choose accessories that match your character.

3 Connect ideas. In Unit 5, you learnt about fashion. In Unit 6, you learnt about combining things to make something new. What connection can you see between the two units?

4 YOU DECIDE Choose an activity.
1. Choose a topic:
   - fashion
   - mash-ups
2. Choose a way to express yourself:
   - a magazine article
   - a fashion show
   - a video
3. Present your work.

Unit 7
Cool Apps and Gadgets

A rider using special LED lights on his bicycle wheels for safety, Hong Kong

'The biggest thing we're trying to do is to make people curious.'
Manu Prakash

TO START

1. Look at the photograph. Why do you think the rider added lights to his bicycle?

2. What electronics are important to you? Which ones do you use every day? Which would you like that you haven't got now?

3. How do you think the electronics you use now will change in the future?

1 More and more people have begun to use electronic gadgets. Why do you think this is?
Discuss. Then listen and read. 🎧 088

It's incredible to think that people haven't even been using the **Internet** for 30 years. When the Internet was first used, you had to **connect** through a telephone line and it could be very slow. Things have changed a lot since then. Today nearly four billion people have a **mobile gadget**, such as a **smartphone**, or a tablet or both. And with **Wi-Fi** in many public spaces, it's easier than ever to connect.

Many agree that mobile gadgets and the **apps** on them are **useful**. They make our lives so much easier. We can do things like **search** for a word in the dictionary or use a torch with just the swipe of a finger! At any time and place, we can **send** and receive e-mails, play **games** or **look up** information. We can also **share** photos and videos or **chat** with friends and family using mobile technology. Smartphones have made it possible to send texts. By 2015, people were sending eight trillion texts per year. It's now the most popular way to communicate.

Because it's so useful, people spend a lot of time on the Internet. Probably too much time! In fact, the average person is online for almost four and a half hours each day. We connect to the Internet with a smartphone more than any other device. Some people worry that we spend too much time with our gadgets. What about you? Do you spend too much time on the Internet?

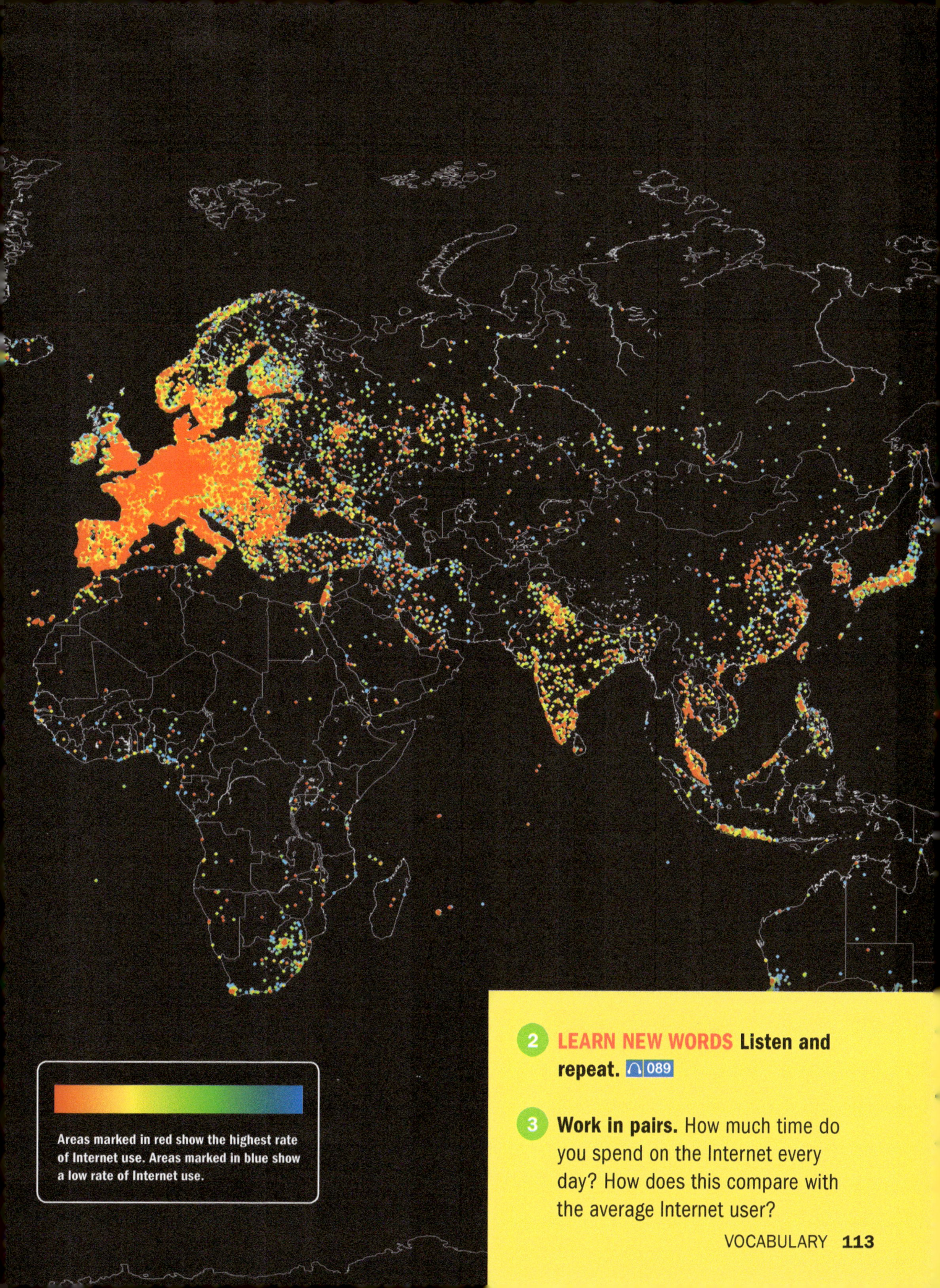

Areas marked in red show the highest rate of Internet use. Areas marked in blue show a low rate of Internet use.

2 **LEARN NEW WORDS** Listen and repeat. 089

3 **Work in pairs.** How much time do you spend on the Internet every day? How does this compare with the average Internet user?

VOCABULARY **113**

4 Read and circle the correct word.

Biophysicist Manu Prakash *connected / sent* to science as a child. He and his brother would spend time in an empty chemistry lab making their own fireworks or electronics. Today, Manu works to make sure that everyone has access to science. He says, 'You can have a kid walking around with a *smartphone / Wi-Fi* who doesn't know that the human body is made of cells.'

Manu wants to *share / look up* his love of science with others. So he helped create a computer powered by water and a low-cost chemistry set. Another amazing *Wi-Fi / gadget* Manu created is the *Foldscope*, a paper microscope. People can make it themselves by folding a special piece of paper. It's small and cheap. The Foldscope is very *useful / chat* for doctors who work in rural areas. They can use them to test for about 20 different diseases. Manu wants children to use them, too. Instead of just *looking up / sending* all their information on the Internet, children can 'walk around with a microscope in their hands' to learn about the world around them.

Manu Prakash sharing his Foldscope with a young girl

5 LEARN NEW WORDS Listen to these words and match them to the clues.
Then listen and repeat. 090 091

| incredible | possible | tablet | text |

_____ 1. It's like a smartphone but bigger.

_____ 2. Something so amazing, we think it can't be true.

_____ 3. This means that something might happen.

_____ 4. We send and receive this with our mobile gadgets.

6 YOU DECIDE Choose an activity.

1. **Work independently.** Think of a tool that can be changed so that it's cheaper and easier to use. Why would changing it be useful? Write a paragraph to explain your idea.

2. **Work in pairs.** What would you like an app to help you do at home? List three things and explain how an app could help.

3. **Work in groups.** Research a new app or gadget that a lot of people don't know about. Explain what it does and how it helps people. Present your research to the class.

SPEAKING STRATEGY 092

Making requests	Responding to requests
May I borrow your <u>tablet</u>?	Of course. Here you are!
Can you lend me your <u>smartphone</u>?	Sure. Here you go.
Please let me use your <u>dictionary</u>.	Sorry. I need it myself.
	I'm sorry. I'm using it <u>at the moment</u>.
	I'm not allowed to lend it out. Sorry!

1 Listen. How do the speakers make and respond to requests? Write the phrases you hear. 093

2 Read and complete the dialogue.

Jun: I forgot my electronic translator. _____ yours?

Chin-Sun: I haven't got one. I just use an app to translate words. Look!

Jun: That's cool. _____ your phone for a few minutes?

Chin-Sun: _____ . Here you go. Oh wait, I need the calculator app for my maths homework.

Jun: No problem. I've got a calculator in my bag.

Chin-Sun: Please _____ .

Jun: _____ . Here you are!

Chin-Sun: Thanks. Wow! This calculator is better than my calculator app!

Jun: Yeah, it *is* good.

Chin-Sun: _____ this calculator for the weekend?

Jun: _____ this weekend. I've got a big maths test on Monday.

3 Work as a class. Choose a card: A, B, C or D. Request the items on your card from your classmates. Respond to their requests. Answer *yes* if the item requested is on your card and *no* if it is not.

STUDENT A: video game | translator | pen | skateboard | watch

Could you lend me your video game?

Go to page 169.

Sorry. I'm using it at the moment.

4 Work in groups. Place five things from your pockets or school bags on your desk. Take turns asking to borrow those items and responding.

SPEAKING **115**

GRAMMAR 094

Superlatives: Talking about extremes

The newest version of this game is going to be amazing.

This puzzle app isn't **the most difficult** one I've got.

This new word game isn't **the most fun** game I've played, but it isn't **the least fun** either.

This action game is **the best**. It has incredible graphics.

The worst game is the card game. It's so boring!

1 **Listen.** Circle all the superlatives you hear. 095

the scariest	the loudest	the most powerful	the highest
the cleverest	the most difficult	the most awful	the coolest
the least boring	the best	the most fun	the least expensive

2 **Work in pairs.** Complete the sentences with the superlative of the words in brackets.

Today, music games are some of _____ (+/popular) games on the Internet. In one game, you can create your own hits in _____ (+/easy) way possible. _____ (+/exciting) thing is that you can create original songs or mash-ups of famous songs. Don't worry! Even _____ (–/musical) person can create amazing songs. _____ (+/good) feature of the game is that you can sing with the music you create! The game makes even _____ (–/bad) singer sound great! _____ (+/important) thing to remember is to share your hits with your friends.

3 **Work in pairs.** Talk about the best and worst video games. Why do you like them? Use superlatives.

> The most interesting games make you solve puzzles.

④ **LEARN NEW WORDS** Listen to learn about some pretty unusual apps. Then listen and repeat. 🎧 096 097

There's an app for that!?!

Your smartphone's **microphone** can tell you if a melon is ready to eat.

Blow into your phone's microphone to create steam on the **screen**. Then you can write in the steam with your finger.

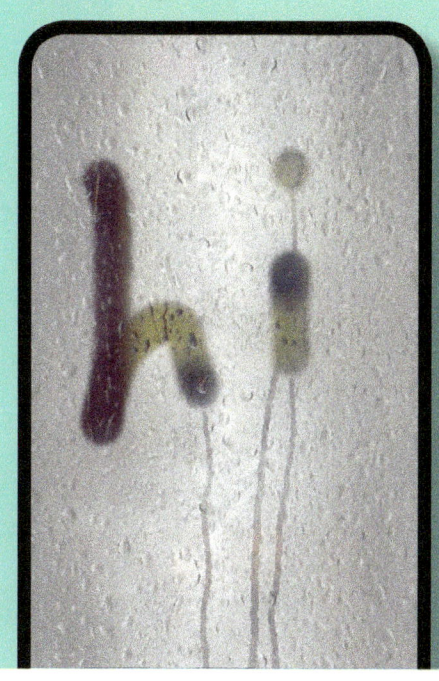

Safely walk as you type into your phone's **keyboard**. The phone's **camera** shows what's in front of you. Be careful: this app uses up your phone's **battery** very quickly!

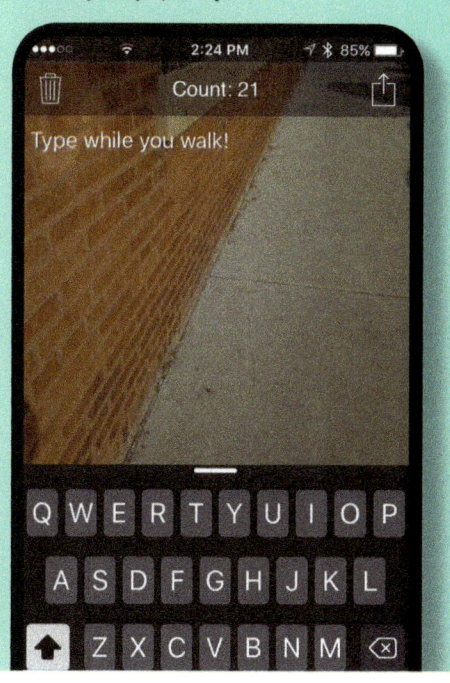

⑤ **Work in pairs.** Complete the sentences using the words in the box. Then say whether you agree or disagree, and why.

> I don't agree with number 5. I record things I need to remember every day.

| battery | camera | keyboard | microphone | screen |

1. A smartphone _____ is the quickest and the easiest way to take pictures.

2. Finding a place to charge your phone's _____ is always easy.

3. Typing on a smartphone's small _____ is the most difficult thing about sending texts.

4. One of the best things about a mobile gadget is that, if you want to, you can see friends on the _____ while you're talking to them.

5. One of the least-used features on a mobile gadget is the _____ .

⑥ **Discuss in groups.** Which apps are the most useful, the most difficult and the most fun? Which are the least useful, the least difficult and the least fun?

GRAMMAR 117

Thinking Outside the BOX

Young inventor Brooke Martin on the screen of an iCPooch

1 BEFORE YOU READ Discuss in pairs. Look at the photo. Describe what you think the gadget does.

2 LEARN NEW WORDS Find these words in the reading. What do you think they mean? Think about what type of word each one is. Then listen and repeat. 🎧 098

borrow	find
function	invent

3 WHILE YOU READ Look for the main idea and details that support it. 🎧 099

4 AFTER YOU READ Work in pairs. Tick T for *true* statements or F for *false*.

1. All you need for Bot2Karot is a smartphone app. Ⓣ Ⓕ
2. Bot2Karot helps people take care of their gardens. Ⓣ Ⓕ
3. Brooke Martin was sixteen when she invented iCPooch. Ⓣ Ⓕ
4. The only thing you can do with iCPooch is look at your dog. Ⓣ Ⓕ
5. Robert Saunt likes playing video games. Ⓣ Ⓕ
6. Robert's gadget will be good for the environment. Ⓣ Ⓕ

Creative teens can make a difference!

If you think young people can't have an impact on the world, think again. Over the years, teens have invented remarkable things that solve problems and have changed the way people do things. And they're going to continue to invent things in the future.

Take 14-year-old Eliott Sarrey from France, for example. He invented Bot2Karot, a gardening robot that can take care of a small vegetable garden. The robot is controlled by an app on a smartphone. It helps people grow and take care of vegetables. It also saves water and energy, and makes gardening easy for people who are very busy or have difficulty getting around.

Brooke Martin is an animal lover who missed her dog when she was away. She also knew that her dog suffered from stress when its owners left. So Brooke invented iCPooch® when she was just 12 years old. The iCPooch lets pet owners check on their pets from anywhere in the world using a tablet or a smartphone. This award-winning gadget also allows owners to use their smartphone camera to video chat with their pets. It has another function, too. Owners can quickly and easily give their pet a treat by touching the *drop treat* button on their screen. Dogs and owners must be pretty grateful to Brooke for this invention!

Fourteen-year-old inventor Robert Saunt was tired of buying or borrowing different video-game controllers for each game console. So he invented a controller called *Game Blox*. It can be used with four of the most popular game consoles. His invention will save players a lot of money and space, and it will save 330 million kg. (727 million lb.) of materials every year. Players will also be able to listen to music while they play video games with Robert's gadget.

Youngsters all over the world find ways to solve problems every day. Who knows? Maybe the next time you have a problem, you'll come up with the next amazing idea!

5 **Discuss your answers to Activity 3 in small groups.** Then complete the following:

Main idea
_____
_____

Detail 1
_____
_____

Detail 2
_____
_____

Detail 3
_____
_____

6 **Discuss in groups.**

1. Which of these three inventions do you think is the most useful? Why? Which do you think is the least useful? Why?
2. What do you think is the greatest invention of all time? Who invented it? Why is it so great?
3. Brooke worried about her dog when she was on holiday. Think of two other ways she could check on her dog while she's away.

VIDEO

1 **BEFORE YOU WATCH Discuss in pairs.** Before smartphones and other new electronic gadgets, how did people tell the time? Take photos? Listen to music?

2 **Read and circle.** You're going to watch *From Gadgets to Apps*. From the title, predict the main idea of the video. Circle the letter.

a. Gadgets are more important than their apps.
b. Useful apps are replacing gadgets.
c. We will use different gadgets and apps in the future.

3 **WHILE YOU WATCH Complete the table. Watch scene 7.1.**

Function	Today	What people first used for this function	The problem with the original gadget
tell the time	clock app		
listen to music	music app		
take a photo	camera app		

4 **AFTER YOU WATCH Match the two parts of the sentences.**

_____ 1. The digital age

_____ 2. Watches in the 1950s

_____ 3. Before there were instant cameras, people

_____ 4. Instant cameras

_____ 5. In the 1950s, gadgets for listening to music

a. were easy to use but only made one copy of a photo.

b. were small and portable but had only one use.

c. were smaller than before, but they still couldn't fit in our pockets.

d. actually began in the 1950s.

e. depended on professional photographers.

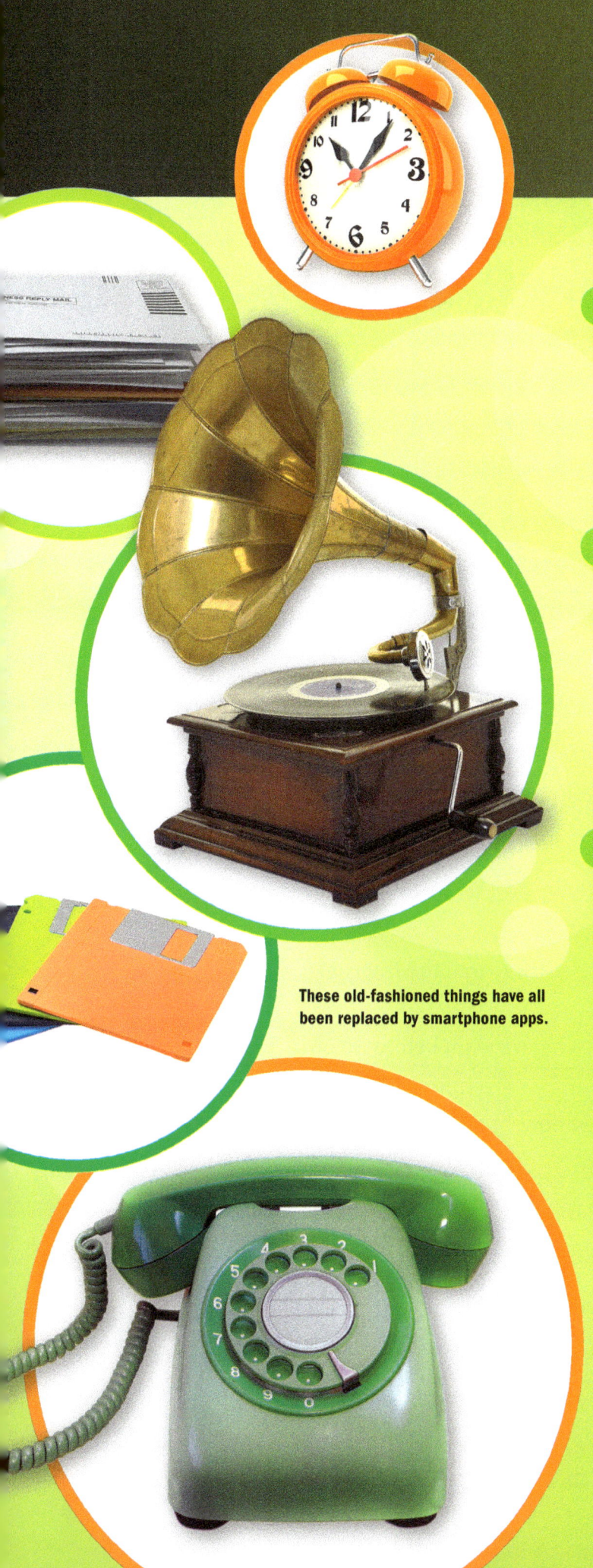

These old-fashioned things have all been replaced by smartphone apps.

5 **Work in pairs.** In the video, you heard, 'Your phone might have an app for giving you directions to a friend's house, but you can't ride it there.' Think of three apps you like. What things can they do? What can't they do? Discuss.

6 **Discuss in groups.**

1. At the end of the video, you're asked, 'What other gadgets do you use? Why are they useful? Will there ever be apps for them?' Answer these questions.
2. What old-fashioned item or gadget is still used in your home? Why is it useful?

7 **YOU DECIDE** Choose an activity.

1. **Work independently.** Find out about the lives of people in your country one hundred years ago. How did they communicate? Travel from place to place? Take photos? Get information? Share what you learn with the class.

2. **Work in pairs.** Role-play a historical figure and a teenager of today. The teen must show and explain how a certain gadget works. The historical figure must react and ask questions appropriate for his/her time period.

3. **Work in groups.** Choose an activity that you do on your smartphone, such as listening to music or taking photos. Use the Internet to find out about how this activity was done at different times in the past. Make a timeline to show how the activity has changed.

VIDEO

GRAMMAR 🎧 100

***Will* and *going to*: Talking about the future**

Possible

We **will have** little machines in our heads that can connect to gadgets.

People **won't talk** to each other on smartphones anymore.

Will people **need** to have so many gadgets?

No, they **won't**. One gadget **will be** all you need.

Most likely

Everything at home **is going to connect** to a gadget.

People **aren't going to use** phones with keyboards anymore.

How are our gadgets **going to help** us every day?

They**'re going to help** us do chores, like watering the garden.

1 **Listen and write the future forms.** 🎧 101

1. _____ have to
2. _____ attach
3. _____ recognise
4. _____ connect
5. _____ swallow
6. _____ take
7. _____ send
8. _____ be

2 **Work in pairs.** Complete the sentences about the future of Internet communication.

1. How is the Internet _____ (change) in the future?
2. We _____ (not have to) search the Internet for what we want.
3. It _____ (know) what we want before we do.
4. All companies are _____ (study) what people do on the Internet even more than they do now.
5. The companies _____ (tell) us what they think we need.

A wearable password

3 **Work in pairs.** Throw a coin and move ahead (heads = 1 space; tails = 2 spaces). When you land on a space, make a prediction about the topic.

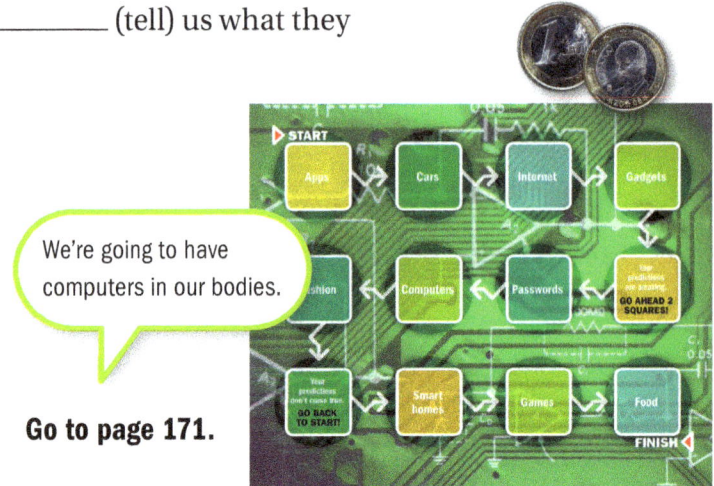

> We're going to have computers in our bodies.

Go to page 171.

122 GRAMMAR

WRITING

When we write a product review, we describe a product. We give examples of what's good and what's bad about it. We can use adjectives to help the reader understand our opinions.

1 Read the model. Work in pairs to find the good and bad points about the product. Underline the good points. Circle the bad points.

Do you like the smell of cakes baking? Fresh flowers? Well, it's now possible to experience these great smells electronically. You just need a cool new gadget for sending smells, scent pellets, and an app on your smartphone or tablet.

This product is amazing because it lets you share smells with people anywhere in the world. Sharing smells can help us connect to an idea or an experience better than just looking at a photo or reading a text. Think about it: you're making biscuits. You take a photo of the biscuits using the app. Then you tag the photo with certain smells, like chocolate or butter. You can combine tags to create more than 300,000 different smells! I love how the product lets you be creative in mixing different scents. I also like the idea of receiving smells. So if my friends are camping and I'm not there, at least I can smell the burning campfire!

This product is incredible, but there are some things about it that I don't like. First, the gadget is big and not very mobile. It would be great to receive smells wherever I go. The company is working on this problem. They're creating bracelets and smartphone cases that will let users receive smells, but these products aren't available yet. The product is also pretty expensive! It may be a while before a lot of people have them, so there won't be many people to share smells with. All in all, I give this product three out of five stars!

2 Discuss in pairs. Would you like to try this product? Why or why not?

3 Write. Write a paragraph to review a product that you have used. Give examples of what you like and don't like about it. Use adjectives to help your readers understand your opinion.

People can send scents by tagging photos, and receive them using this tabletop device.

WRITING 123

Always Keep Learning

'It's valuable to know what you don't know, and there's so much we don't know.'

Manu Prakash
National Geographic Explorer, Biophysicist

1. **Watch scene 7.2.**

2. Manu made a microscope that was cheap and easy to carry. How could this microscope be useful to a student like you? What could you learn if you had access to a microscope wherever you were?

3. Name something that you're interested in but don't know a lot about. What would you like to learn about it? How could you learn this information?

124 MISSION

Make an Impact

YOU DECIDE Choose a project.

1 **Plan and give a presentation about the future.**

- Take photos of five things in your house that you think we won't use or that will be very different ten years from now.
- Prepare a presentation about what will replace these things or how they'll change and why.
- Present your ideas to the class.

2 **Design a robot.**

- Think about a task you don't like doing. Design a robot to do that task.
- Draw and label a picture of your robot.
- Present your robot to the class. Explain how it will work.

3 **Create an 'outdated gadget museum'.**

- Collect five or six items that were useful in the past but have been replaced by smartphones.
- Arrange the items in a 'museum'. Write descriptions of the items, including when they were invented and when they became less popular.
- Display your museum in class. Answer your classmates' questions about each item.

This solar-powered 'tree' uses energy from the sun to charge the batteries of different mobile gadgets.

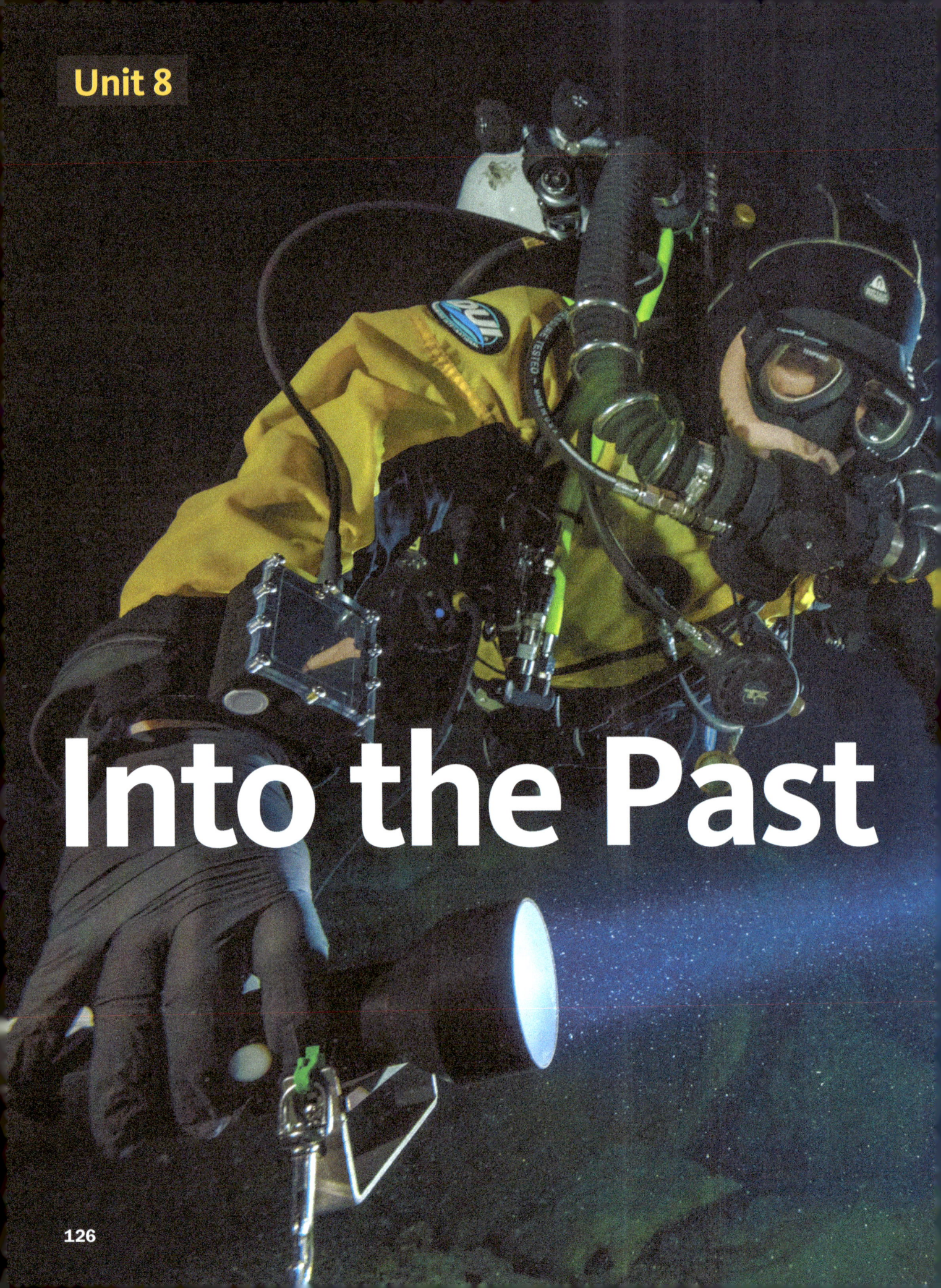

Unit 8

Into the Past

'It's human nature to explore and learn about ourselves by searching for clues of the past.'
                    Alberto Nava Blank

In the Hoyo Negro cenote in Mexico, divers Alberto Nava Blank and Susan Bird find the skull of Naia, a teenage girl who lived approximately 13,000 years ago.

TO START

1. Look at the photo. How are the divers going 'into the past'?

2. Why do you think researchers try to understand the past?

3. Are you interested in learning about people who lived before you? Why or why not?

127

1 Look at the pictures from Nasca in Peru. What can archaeology tell us about the past? Discuss. Then listen and read. 🎧 102

For centuries, archaeologists and anthropologists have searched for information about the **origins** of the mysterious lines drawn in the desert sands of southern Peru. There are approximately 300 different figures – called geoglyphs – and 70 designs showing different **species** of animals and plants.

Scientists **believe** that these geoglyphs were created by the Nasca people, an ancient civilisation living near the modern town of Nasca. The Nasca people lived from about 200 BCE and survived for almost eight centuries, living along river valleys and cultivating crops such as cotton and important foods for their **diet**, like beans and corn. Indeed, some scientists think that some of the geoglyphs date back even earlier and were made by the **ancestors** of the Nasca people – the Paracas people who date back to approximately 800 BCE.

In addition to the Nasca lines, archaeologists **discovered** an impressive village **site** called Cahuachi with an adobe pyramid, large temples, plazas, and staircases and corridors. They also found smaller items like pottery, textiles and some traces of gold.

128 VOCABULARY

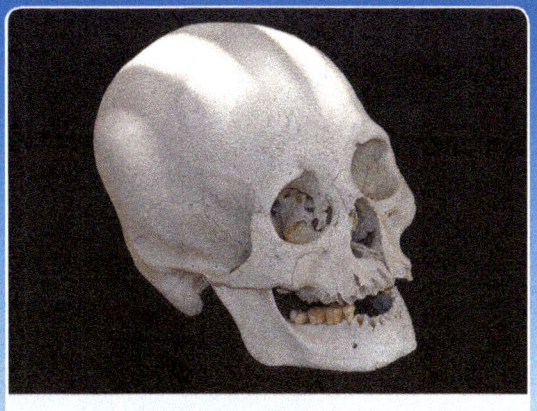

In the same area, scientists excavated the **bones** of **adults** and children and even entire **skeletons**.

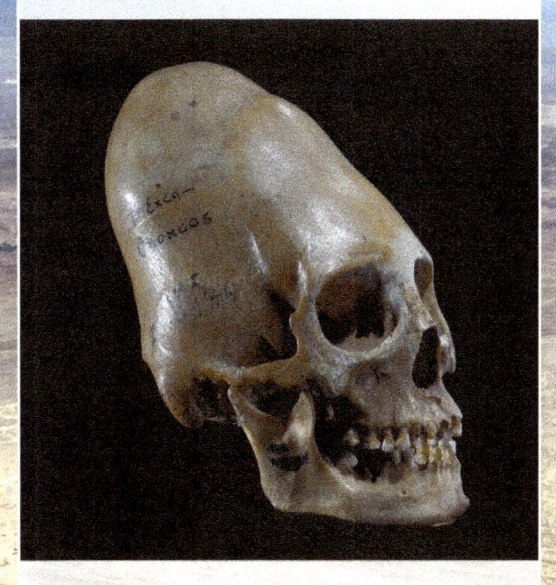

In some cases, the **skulls** were shaped differently and made longer; scientists believe this was done by binding an infant's skull between two pieces of wood. It is thought that this practice showed who belonged to the upper classes in Nasca society.

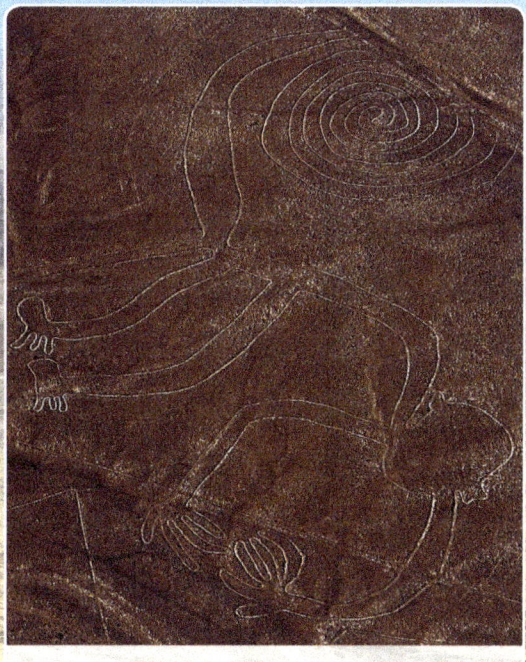

Since 1994, the area has been designated a UNESCO World Heritage Site. This means it is protected, and future generations will **continue** to learn about the **civilisation** and, importantly, enjoy the mysteries of the Nasca.

2   **LEARN NEW WORDS** Listen and repeat. 🎧 103

3   **Work in pairs.** Why do you think it's important to understand our ancestors? Name at least two reasons.

VOCABULARY   **129**

4 Read and write the words from the list. Make any necessary changes.

| adult | ancestor | believe | bone | civilisation |
| discover | origin | site | skull | species |

Alberto Nava Blank

Alberto Nava Blank is an underwater cave explorer. In 2007, Alberto and his team _____ the skeleton of a young girl in the Hoyo Negro cenote in Mexico's Yucatán Peninsula. 'The moment we entered the _____ , we knew it was an incredible place,' says Alberto. They named the girl Naia. Her skeleton had all of the most important _____ , including the _____ with some teeth still in it. Scientists don't think that Naia was an _____ . They _____ she was about 13 when she died around 13,000 years ago. They think that her _____ came from an ancient _____ that lived in north-east Asia.

5 LEARN NEW WORDS Listen to these words and complete the sentences. Then listen and repeat. 🎧 104 105

Ötzi at age 45

| advanced | back | descendant | helpful |

1. Our ancestors go _____ millions of years.
2. They used less- _____ tools than we do today.
3. Scientists have found 19 of Ötzi's _____ .
4. Fossils are _____ in understanding the past.

6 YOU DECIDE Choose an activity.

1. **Work independently.** Find out about an archaeological discovery in your country. What was discovered? What does it tell you about life long ago? Write a paragraph to describe what you learnt.

2. **Work in pairs.** Research Ötzi to learn more about his appearance, habits, habitat and diet. Create a poster profile of the Ice Man.

3. **Work in groups.** Research the discovery of a different primitive species. Where was it discovered? Who discovered it? What did scientists learn? Present the information to the class.

VOCABULARY

SPEAKING STRATEGY 🎧 106

Talking about likes and dislikes

I'm really into <u>history</u>. <u>History</u> is amazing.
I don't mind <u>studying history</u>. It's OK. / It's not bad.
I don't like <u>tests</u> at all. <u>Tests</u> are awful.

Kabuki performers

1 **Listen.** How do the speakers talk about likes and dislikes? Write the phrases you hear. 🎧 107

2 **Read and complete the dialogue.**

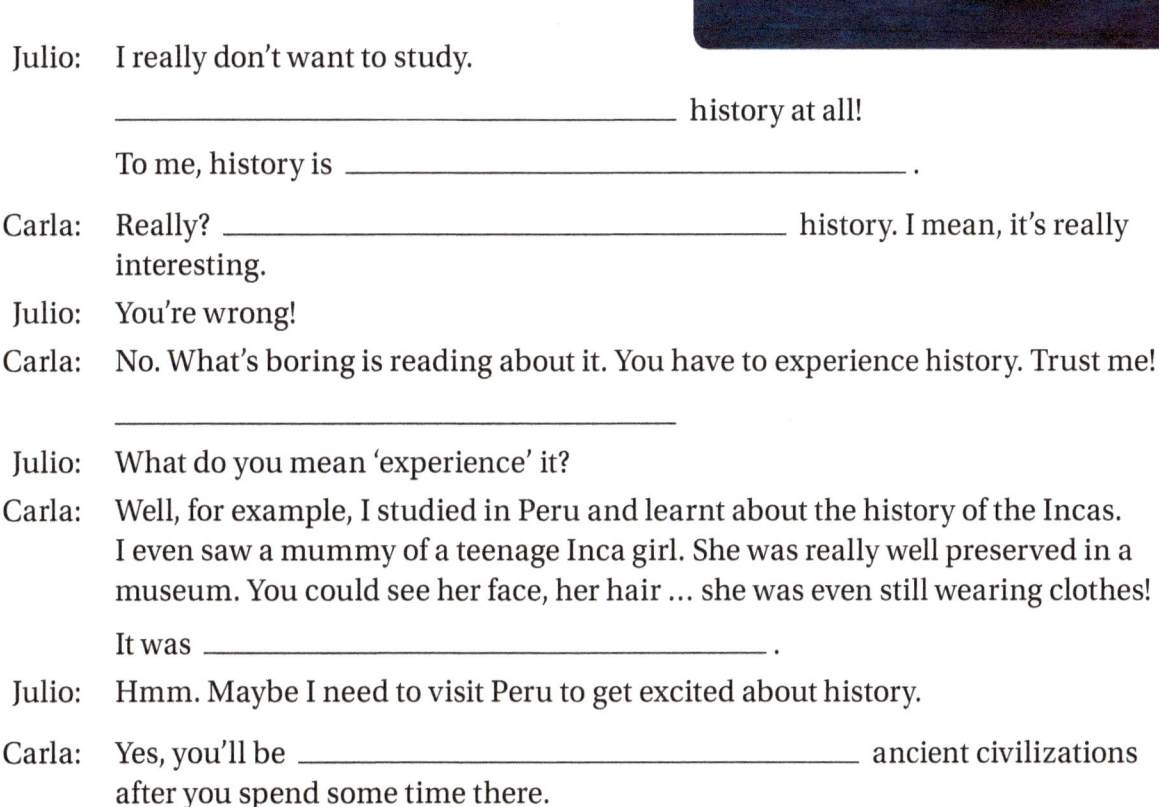

Julio: I really don't want to study.
_____ history at all!
To me, history is _____ .

Carla: Really? _____ history. I mean, it's really interesting.

Julio: You're wrong!

Carla: No. What's boring is reading about it. You have to experience history. Trust me!
_____

Julio: What do you mean 'experience' it?

Carla: Well, for example, I studied in Peru and learnt about the history of the Incas. I even saw a mummy of a teenage Inca girl. She was really well preserved in a museum. You could see her face, her hair … she was even still wearing clothes!
It was _____ .

Julio: Hmm. Maybe I need to visit Peru to get excited about history.

Carla: Yes, you'll be _____ ancient civilizations after you spend some time there.

3 **Work in pairs.** Play Noughts and Crosses. Discuss things you like and dislike. Mark X or O. Try to get three in a row.

I'm really into singing.

I'm really into …	I don't mind …	I don't like … at all.
… is OK, but … is awful.	wild	… is OK.
… is amazing.	… is not bad.	… is awful.

Go to page 173.

4 **Discuss in pairs.** When is it acceptable to use the phrases above to talk about likes and dislikes? When is it not acceptable? What can you say instead of words like *amazing* and *awful* in more formal situations?

SPEAKING 131

GRAMMAR 108

Present perfect: Describing a past action that still continues

Games **have** always **been** a popular activity.

People **have enjoyed** games **for** thousands of years.

People **haven't played** board games as much **since** video games became popular.

Why has this game **become** so popular?

Have many games **changed** over time? **Yes**, they **have**.

1 **Listen.** Are the actions completed or continuing? Tick the correct column. 109

	Completed	Continuing
play		
say		
begin		
enjoy		
go		
take		

People have played mancala for thousands of years.

2 **Work in pairs.** Complete the sentences. Use the present perfect forms of the verbs in brackets, and *for* or *since* where appropriate.

1. People _____ (play) mancala _____ thousands of years.

2. Players _____ (enjoy) different versions of mancala _____ ancient times.

3. _____ the 1980s, players _____ (use) computers to play mancala.

4. Players _____ (create) about two hundred different mancala games.

5. Many players _____ (not play) mancala with seeds or stones _____ computers became popular.

3 **Discuss in groups.** What's your favourite game? Why? Who has played it with you? How often have you played it? How many times have you won?

> My favourite board game is Scrabble™. My dad and I have played it every week since I got it.

132 GRAMMAR

4 **LEARN NEW WORDS** Listen to learn about the history of chess.
Then listen and repeat. 🎧 110 111

The queen became the most powerful chess **piece** on the board in the 1500s.

You can checkmate him in four moves!

King Ferdinand and **Queen** Isabella of Spain played **chess**. Isabella gave Ferdinand **advice** on how to win the game.

5 **Work independently.** Complete the sentences using the words in the box. Make any necessary changes.

advice	chess	piece	queen

1. People have played _____ for about 1,400 years.

2. It's played on a board with 32 _____ .

3. In a chess game, no one should give a player _____ on how to move.

4. The _____ is a very powerful piece in chess.

6 **Work in groups.** Find out about other popular games. Discuss them using the present perfect.

People in China have played *Go* for hundreds of years.

GRAMMAR **133**

Growing Up: THEN AND NOW

How children's lives have changed over the years

1. **BEFORE YOU READ** **Discuss in pairs.** Look at the girl in the photo. How do you think her life was different from yours?

2. **LEARN NEW WORDS** Find these words in the reading. What do you think they mean? Look for their definitions or examples in the text. Then listen and repeat. 🎧 112

   | age | chore | education | teenager |

3. **WHILE YOU READ** Think about cause and effect. 🎧 113

4. **AFTER YOU READ** Work in pairs to answer the questions.
   1. What culture thought that education was very important?
   2. Why couldn't some parents teach their children at home?
   3. At what age did children learn to weave?
   4. How often did children work in factories?
   5. At what age did children begin working in factories?
   6. What did children do with the money they earned?

5. **Complete the table.**

Cause	Effect
	Most children didn't go to school from 500–1500.
Aztecs believed that education was important.	
	Children began working in factories in cities.

6. **Work in groups.**
   1. What would be the hardest thing for you if you were growing up in the past? Why?
   2. Interview an older person about his or her life as a teenager. How was it the same as your life now? How was it different?
   3. Why do you think the lives of children around the world have improved from long ago? Give three reasons. Do you think it's worse in any way today? Explain.

134 READING

What's a day in your life like today? You probably go to school and do your homework. At home, you do a few simple chores, like doing the washing up or making your bed. You might complain about not having enough free time to relax.

In the past, children your age probably had a little more to complain about. Throughout much of history, many didn't go to school because they had to help all day at home or on the farm. Their parents taught them what they knew, but very few adults could read or write. The Aztec people, who lived from 1200 to 1473 in present-day Mexico, were unique. The Aztecs believed that education, or learning, was important. Every child went to school, although boys and girls learnt different things.

In addition to going to school, Aztec children were expected to help with chores at home. Girls learnt to weave at the age of about four, and they learnt to cook at the age of about 12. Boys, on the other hand, learnt occupational skills.

By the 19th century, many people began moving into cities to find jobs. In cities, there was no longer a need to have children work on the farm. So they began working in factories instead. In England, many children worked long hours six days a week. And they earned very little money in return. Children started working from a very young age, sometimes at only five or six years old. They gave all of their money to their parents to help pay for the family's needs.

Today, most children go to school. Sometimes teenagers work part-time jobs to earn money. But many use that money for enjoyment, not to help their families. Think about it! Even if you work and go to school, you still have time to relax or spend time with your friends. Next to children from the past, most children nowadays have it pretty easy!

A girl working in a factory, 1908

VIDEO ▶

4.5 billion years ago
The Earth forms.

230 million years ago
The earliest known dinosaurs are living on Earth.

100 million years ago
Spinosaurus lives in the Sahara region. At this time, the Sahara is a river system, not a desert.

65 million years ago
The last dinosaurs (except birds) become extinct.

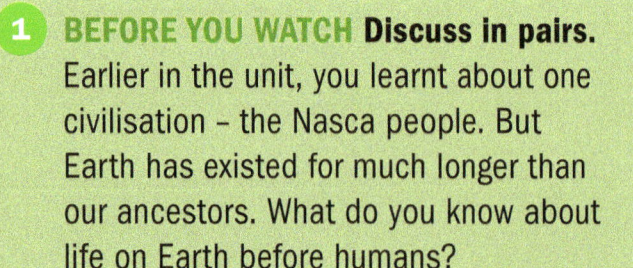

1 BEFORE YOU WATCH Discuss in pairs. Earlier in the unit, you learnt about one civilisation – the Nasca people. But Earth has existed for much longer than our ancestors. What do you know about life on Earth before humans?

2 Work in pairs. You are going to watch *A Journey Back in Time*. The explorer Nizar Ibrahim makes a discovery about life before humans. Look at the photo of Nizar (the last photo on the timeline). What do you think he discovered?

3 WHILE YOU WATCH Check your predictions from Activity 2. Watch scene 8.1.

4 AFTER YOU WATCH Work in pairs to answer the questions.

1. Today the Sahara Desert is full of sand. What was it like 100 million years ago?
2. What was Nizar looking for?
3. Where did he work? Why did people think he was foolish to work there?
4. He found part of a skeleton. What type of creature did it belong to?
5. During the time of dinosaurs, what important group was **not** on Earth?

2.5 million years ago

Our human ancestors begin using stone tools, a sign of advanced intelligence.

5,000 years ago

Ötzi, the Ice Man, lived in the Alps. He used tools such as axes and knives.

2,300 years ago

The Nasca people created the mysterious 'Nasca lines' in Peru.

Present-day

Modern humans have the tools and technology to study and understand the past.

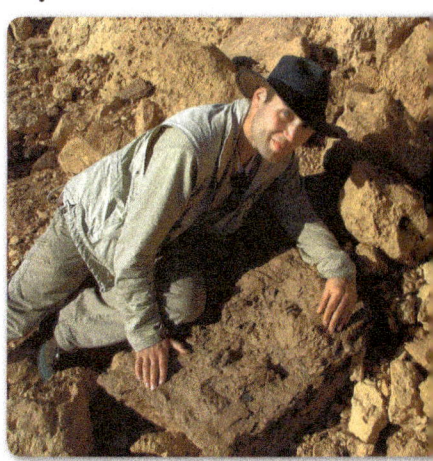

5 Discuss in pairs.

1. Look at the timeline. How many years separate the last dinosaurs from the present day? What do you think happened during this period?

2. Nizar says that holding dinosaur fossils is like holding 'a snapshot in time'. What would be exciting about holding something so old?

6 YOU DECIDE Choose an activity.

1. **Work independently.** Nizar describes the Sahara as 'a magical place, both beautiful and frightening, peaceful and cruel'. Think of another place that is beautiful and peaceful, but can still be frightening. Describe this place to the class. If possible, share a photo.

2. **Work in pairs.** In the video, Nizar imagines the world when dinosaurs lived. Discuss how you imagine the world at this time. Draw a picture and share it with the class.

3. **Work in groups.** Create a short story or comic book about life during the time of the dinosaurs. Share your work with the class.

GRAMMAR 🎧 114

***There + to be*: Expressing existence at different points of time**

There have always **been** sun celebrations around the world.

However, **there wasn't** a Festival of the Sun in Peru between 1535 and 1944.

Now **there's** a Festival of the Sun every year.

Are there going to be traditional musicians?

Will there be a lot of people?

There has been a Festival of the Sun in Peru for centuries.

There weren't any other traditional Incan festivals at that time either.

There are a lot of different foods to try.

Yes, **there are going to be** dancers, too.

I think **there will be**. It's very popular.

1 **Read and complete the dialogue.** Use *there* + the correct form of *to be*.

Juan: Andrea, you're from Peru, aren't you? _____ a lot of fun things to do during your country's Festival of the Sun?

Andrea: Yes, _____ . The festival is called *Inti Raymi*. It's a week long, and _____ live concerts and shows. In fact, _____ only one festival in South America that's bigger!

An Inti Raymi celebration

Juan: Really? It sounds amazing!

Andrea: Oh, it is. Last year _____ about 150,000 people in the town of Cuzco watching the ceremony. _____ 500 actors in the ceremony. They really brought the past to life.

Juan: Cool! Does the history of this festival go back a long time?

Andrea: Oh, yes! _____ Inti Raymi celebrations since the 1400s.

Juan: _____ a festival next year?

Andrea: Yes, _____ . It's held every year.

2 **Work in pairs.** Think of a festival you have been to. Describe the festival with as many details as possible. Use *there* with the correct form of *to be*.

3 **Work in groups.** Choose a celebration you all know about. Turn over a card. Try to be the first to slap the card and make a sentence about that celebration.

There will be …

Go to page 175.

138 GRAMMAR

WRITING

When you write a classification paragraph, you divide your main topic into different parts. You give details and examples about each of the parts. When you finish, write a concluding sentence to connect the parts to the main topic.

1 **Read the model.** What is the main topic? How many parts does the writer divide the paragraph into?

    The summer solstice, the first day of summer, has always been a special day. There have been summer solstice celebrations since ancient times. Some of these are still celebrated today. In Sweden, people celebrate this, the longest day of the year, by singing, dancing around a maypole, and enjoying special food and drinks. Unlike Sweden, people in Spain don't dance around a maypole. Instead, they dance in the streets. There are fireworks and bonfires. Some people even jump over the bonfires. People in both Sweden and Spain celebrate the summer solstice at the end of the day. However, at Stonehenge, in the United Kingdom, thousands of people come together to celebrate the longest day of the year at sunrise. The sounds of beating drums fill the air at this celebration. People around the world celebrate the summer solstice in different ways that reflect their culture.

2 **Work in pairs.** What are the different parts of the paragraph? What does the writer describe in each part?

3 **Write.** Write a paragraph about a traditional festival or celebration from your culture. Write three details or examples and a concluding sentence.

A summer solstice celebration at Stonehenge, United Kingdom

Understand the Past

'The underwater caves of the Yucatán Peninsula are a time capsule of what human lives were like 10,000 years ago.'

Alberto Nava Blank
National Geographic Explorer, Underwater Cave Explorer/Cartographer

1. **Watch scene 8.2.**

2. A time capsule is a collection of artefacts that represent a certain period of time. What are three things that you might find in a time capsule from 10,000 years ago? 1,000 years ago? 10 years ago?

3. Think of life in your country 100 years ago. What was harder back then? Was anything better?

Make an Impact

YOU DECIDE Choose a project.

1 **Teach the class to play mancala.**
- Research the history of mancala. Learn how to play. Write the instructions on a poster.
- Make mancala boards for your classmates. Use egg boxes. Bring in seeds or beans as pieces.
- Share your poster and teach classmates how to play mancala. Walk around to answer any questions as others play the game.

2 **Make a biographical poster.**
- Research a scientist who discovered something connected to our origins.
- Prepare a biography of that person. Include information on what he or she discovered and what it taught us about our origins.
- Create a poster and share the information with the class.

3 **Perform a sketch.**
- Choose a time period in the past and research what children did then.
- Write and rehearse a sketch showing what life was like for children at that time. Find costumes and props.
- Perform the sketch for your classmates.

Mancala

1 Read and listen to a student's predictions for the future. 🎧 115

Dear 'future friend',

I'm writing this letter for my school's time capsule. I want to include my predictions for the future instead of describing the present. I love to think about the future, especially how people will get around.

I bet that there will be some cool ways to travel in the future. For example, people will be able to live in one city and work in another because we'll be able to travel in small pods that move really fast – more than 1,200 kph (750 mph) – through a special tunnel. Just like in aeroplanes, there will be screens on the backs of seats so passengers can relax and watch films as they travel. And the best thing will be that the vehicles that travel in this tunnel will use energy from the sun, so they'll be better for the environment.

Transport in the future will do more than just move us around quickly. It will take us out of this world! People are already talking about travelling to Mars. I bet that in the future it will take about four to six months to get there. Then travellers will stay about two years. Of course, going to Mars won't be for everyone. If people just want to look at Earth from above, they'll be able to take a lift into space!

When you read this letter, please check how many of my predictions have come true. Who knows? Maybe I'll be able to time travel to find out myself!

Maria

A space lift

2 **Discuss in groups.**
1. Have you ever seen a time capsule? If so, what was in it? If not, would you be interested in one? Why or why not?
2. What would you put in a time capsule to be opened in 100 years?
3. Which forms of transport that Maria mentions would you like to take? Why?

3 **Connect ideas.** In Unit 7, you learnt about life with modern gadgets. In Unit 8, you learnt about people, tools and games from long ago. What connection can you see between the two units?

4 **YOU DECIDE** **Choose an activity.**
1. Choose a topic:
    - tools and games of today and tomorrow
    - tools and games of the past
2. Choose a way to express yourself:
    - a letter for a time capsule
    - a video presentation
    - a sketch
3. Present your work.

Unit 5

The -ed ending

1 **Listen.** Notice the different pronunciations for each -ed ending. 🎧 127

id	t	d
wanted	looked	enjoyed
needed	dressed	changed
protected	helped	loved

The -ed ending has three possible pronunciations:

- *id* sound when the final sound of a verb is *t* or *d*
- *t* sound when the final sound of a verb is *f, k, p, s, sh, ch* and *x*
- *d* sound when the final sound of a verb is a vowel or any other consonant

2 **Listen and repeat the words.** Then write the number of syllables in each word. 🎧 128

1. _1_ played   4. ___ created   7. ___ needed
2. ___ climbed   5. ___ picked   8. ___ asked
3. ___ waited   6. ___ reached   9. ___ protected

3 **Listen and repeat.** Then write each word in the correct column. Listen to check your answers. 🎧 129 130

~~added~~	attached	believed	coloured
decided	dried	graduated	mixed
produced	saved	washed	wasted

id	t	d
added		

Unit 6

Linking: Consonant + vowel sounds

1 **Listen.** Notice how the words join together. 🎧 131

Who is it?

I give up.

It's got the body of a lion.

When a word ending in a consonant sound comes before a word beginning with a vowel sound, the final consonant sound often links to the vowel. It sounds like one long word.

2 **Listen and repeat.** Draw a link from the final consonant sound to the vowel. 🎧 132

1. It's amazing!   4. was it   7. planned anything
2. made up   5. think I   8. What's up?
3. have a   6. love it

3 **Work in pairs.** Complete the conversation with phrases from Activity 2. Listen to check your answers. 🎧 133

Jane: Hi, Kim! ___What's up?___

Kim: I just _____ a poem in my drama exam.

Jane: How _____ ?

Kim: Difficult! I _____ passed, though.

Jane: That's good. So have you _____ for your birthday yet?

Kim: Not yet. I want to _____ party at the new Korean restaurant. Do you like karaoke?

Jane: I _____ ! What's Korean food like?

Kim: _____

146 Pronunciation

Unit 7
The two-vowel rule

1 **Listen.** Notice how the vowels in these words are pronounced like the first vowel. 🎧 134

a	e	i	o	u
p**ai**d	r**ea**d	d**ie**	r**oa**d	d**ue**
b**a**ke	P**e**te	b**i**ke	b**o**ne	t**u**ne

As a rule, when two vowels are in the same word or syllable, the second vowel is silent. The letter name is the sound. For example, in the words *paid* and *bake*, the sound is like the name of the letter *a*.

Although there are exceptions, this is true most of the time.

2 **Listen and repeat.** Circle the word where the two-vowel rule does not work. 🎧 135

1. seat, beach, (great), peach, team
2. save, have, wave, shave, behave
3. some, phone, home, joke, bone
4. oat, soap, road, boat, roar
5. cute, cube, Tuesday, statue, duet
6. train, said, paid, rain, explain

3 **Work in pairs.** Look at pages 112–113. Find words that follow the two-vowel rule. Write as many of them as you can in two minutes.

a	e	i	o	u

Unit 8
The schwa (/ə/) sound

1 **Listen.** Notice the pronunciation of the underlined vowels. 🎧 136

Chin**a**	stud**e**nt	fam**i**ly
t**o**night	helpf**u**l	act**io**n

As you've learnt, when a word in English has two or more syllables, one is stronger, or stressed. The vowel in a stressed syllable is clearly pronounced.

Vowel sounds in unstressed syllables are not fully pronounced and often do not sound like the letter in the word. Many unstressed syllables have the *schwa* sound.

Schwa is a relaxed *uh* sound. The symbol in dictionaries looks like an upside-down *e* (/ə/). Schwa is the most common sound in the English language.

2 **Listen.** Complete the schwa sounds in these words with the missing vowels. Then listen again and repeat. 🎧 137 138

1. I'm really into hist___ry.
2. I made my fam___ly tree because I want to know where I came from.
3. The Ice Man lived in anc___ ___nt times.
4. These days, life is not as diffic___lt for childr___n as it was in the past, but some still c___mplain!
5. J___pan is in As___ ___ .
6. The USA is in North ___meric___ .

3 **Work in pairs.** Listen and repeat these words. Circle the syllables with the schwa sound. Compare your answers. Then take turns saying the words. 🎧 139

(a)go	descen dant	li on
sym bol	festi val	pro ba bly
con trol	na tion	skele ton

Pronunciation **147**

Irregular Verbs

Infinitive	Past simple	Past participle	Infinitive	Past simple	Past participle
be	were	been	leave	left	left
beat	beat	beaten	lend	lent	lent
become	became	become	let	let	let
begin	began	begun	lie (down)	lay	lain
bend	bent	bent	light	lit	lit
bet	bet	bet	lose	lost	lost
bite	bit	bitten	make	made	made
bleed	bled	bled	mean	meant	meant
blow	blew	blown	meet	met	met
break	broke	broken	overcome	overcame	overcome
bring	brought	brought	pay	paid	paid
build	built	built	put	put	put
burn	burnt	burnt	quit	quit	quit
buy	bought	bought	read	read	read
carry	carried	carried	ride	rode	ridden
catch	caught	caught	ring	rang	rung
choose	chose	chosen	rise	rose	risen
come	came	come	run	ran	run
cost	cost	cost	say	said	said
cut	cut	cut	see	saw	seen
deal	dealt	dealt	sell	sold	sold
dig	dug	dug	send	sent	sent
dive	dived	dived	set	set	set
do	did	done	sew	sewed	sewn
draw	drew	drawn	shake	shook	shaken
drink	drank	drunk	shine	shone	shone
drive	drove	driven	show	showed	shown
dry	dried	dried	shrink	shrank	shrunk
eat	ate	eaten	shut	shut	shut
fall	fell	fallen	sing	sang	sung
feed	fed	fed	sink	sank	sunk
feel	felt	felt	sit	sat	sat
fight	fought	fought	sleep	slept	slept
find	found	found	slide	slid	slid
flee	fled	fled	speak	spoke	spoken
fly	flew	flown	spend	spent	spent
forbid	forbade	forbidden	spin	spun	spun
forget	forgot	forgotten	stand	stood	stood
forgive	forgave	forgiven	steal	stole	stolen
freeze	froze	frozen	stick	stuck	stuck
fry	fried	fried	sting	stung	stung
get	got	got	stink	stank	stunk
give	gave	given	strike	struck	struck
go	went	gone	swear	swore	sworn
grind	ground	ground	sweep	swept	swept
grow	grew	grown	swim	swam	swum
hang	hung	hung	swing	swung	swung
have	had	had	take	took	taken
hear	heard	heard	teach	taught	taught
hide	hid	hidden	tear	tore	torn
hit	hit	hit	tell	told	told
hold	held	held	think	thought	thought
hurt	hurt	hurt	throw	threw	thrown
keep	kept	kept	understand	understood	understood
kneel	knelt	knelt	wake	woke	woken
knit	knitted	knitted	wear	wore	worn
know	knew	known	weave	wove	woven
lay	laid	laid	win	won	won
lead	led	led	write	wrote	written

Greetings: Formal and informal

1 **Listen and read.** 🎧 140

Formal

Ben: Hello, Mr Moore. How are you?
Mr Moore: Very well, thank you. And you?

Greeting	Responding
• Hello. How are you? • Good (morning). How are you?	• Very well, thank you. And you? • Fine, thank you. Good (morning). How are you?

2 **Listen and read.** 🎧 141

Informal

Gabi: Hi, Ben. How are you doing?
Ben: I'm OK, thanks. How are you?

Greeting	Responding
• Hi! How are you? • Hello. How's it going? • Hi. How are you doing?	• I'm OK, thanks. • Hi. I'm fine, thanks. How are you? • Great, thanks. How about you? • Not bad, thanks. You?
• Hey. What's happening? • Hey there. What are you up to? • Hey. What's going on?	• Nothing much. • Nothing special. You? • Not much. How about you?

Social and Academic Language **149**

Introductions: Formal and informal

3 **Listen and read.** 🎧 142

Formal

Gabi: Mr Moore, I'd like to introduce you to Ben.
Mr Moore: Hello, Ben. It's a pleasure to meet you.

Making an introduction	Responding
• I'd like you to meet Ben. • I'd like to introduce you to Ben. • Please allow me to introduce Ben. He's a student at my school. • I don't think we've met. May I introduce myself? I'm Ben.	• I'm very pleased to meet you. • It's a pleasure to meet you, Ben. • Hello, Ben. I'm glad to meet you. • Hello, Ben. I'm Mr Moore. Pleased to meet you.

4 **Listen and read.** 🎧 143

Informal

Ben: Hi. My name is Ben. Nice to meet you.
Gabi: Hi, Ben. I'm Gabi. Very nice to meet you, too.

Making an introduction	Responding
• Hi. I'm Ben. • Hi there. My name is Ben. Nice to meet you. • Hi, Ben. This is Gabi. She's in my class. • This is Ben. He's a student in my school.	• Hi, Ben. My name is Gabi. Nice to meet you. • Hello. I'm Gabi. Very nice to meet you, too. • Hi, Gabi. Nice to meet you. • Hi, Ben. I'm Gabi. It's nice to meet you.

Asking for permission

5 **Listen and read.** 🎧 144

Isabella: Mum, can I go to the cinema on Friday after school?
Mum: Sure. Who are you going with? And how are you getting there?
Isabella: I'm going with Mia and Valerie. Is it OK if we walk?
Mum: I'm afraid not. But I can take you.

Asking for permission	Giving permission	Refusing permission
• Can I/we …? • May I/we …? (formal) • Is it OK if I/we …? • Do you mind if I/we …? • Would you mind if …? • Would it be OK if …?	• Sure. • No problem. • Of course. • Go ahead.	• I don't think so. • I'm afraid not. • I'm sorry, but no.

150 Social and Academic Language

Expressing thanks: Formal and informal

6 Listen and read. 🎧 145

Formal

Mr Moore: You've been very helpful. That's very thoughtful of you.
Gabi: Of course. Please don't mention it.

Expressing thanks	Responding
• Thank you. That's very kind of you. • I appreciate your help. • Thank you. That's very thoughtful. • I'm very grateful for (your help).	• It's my pleasure. • It's no trouble at all. • Of course. Please don't mention it. • It was the least I could do. • It was no problem. I'm glad to help.

7 Listen and read. 🎧 146

Informal

Gabi: Wow! That's so nice of you. Thanks a lot.
Ben: You're welcome!

Expressing thanks	Responding
• Thanks. • Thanks a lot. • Thanks very much. • Thanks for (asking).	• You're welcome. • It's nothing! • No problem. • Sure thing. • Any time.

Taking turns

8 Listen and read. 🎧 147

Rika: We have to practise the dialogue on page 86. Who should go first?
Tamiko: Why don't you?
Rika: OK, sure.

Asking	Responding	Agreeing
• Who should go first? • Do you want to say the first line? • Who would like to start?	• Why don't you? • I went first the last time. • I'd like to. • Would it be OK if I went first?	• OK, sure. • Alright. • Sure. Go ahead.

Social and Academic Language **151**

Asking for and giving information

9 **Listen and read.** 🎧 148

Julia: Hey, Carlos. Could you tell me what the maths homework is?
Carlos: As far as I know, we just need to study for the test.
Julia: I wonder what's on it. Do you have any idea?
Carlos: Well, I heard that it's all of Unit 10 and the first part of Unit 11.

Asking for information	Responding
• Can/Could you tell me …? • I'd like to know … • I wonder … • Do you know? • Do you have any idea?	• I heard/read that … • As far as I know, … • I'm not sure, but I think … • I'd say … • I don't know.

Doing a presentation

10 **Listen and read.** 🎧 149

Fatima: Today, we're going to talk about dinosaurs.
Rana: We'll start by describing the different groups of dinosaurs.
Fatima: Have a look at this poster. You'll see that there are many different groups.
Rana: Next, let's look at what dinosaurs ate.
Fatima: As you can see, there's a lot to learn about dinosaurs. Any questions?

Beginning	Middle	End
• Today I'm/we're going to show you … • Today I'm/we're going to talk about … • I'll/We'll start by …	• Take a look at … • You'll see that … • Next, let's look at …	• As you can see, … • Any questions?

Unit 5 Cutouts Use with Activity 3 on page 81.

Start

End

Our clothes **show/don't show** who we really are.

We **should/shouldn't** be allowed to wear jeans to school.

You shared a lot of opinions. **Congratulations!**

Casual clothes **should/shouldn't** replace formal clothes in all situations.

You didn't wear your school uniform today. **Lose a turn!**

Fashion **will/won't** change much in the next century.

Boys **should/shouldn't** wear ties to school.

Dressing up **is/isn't** fun.

Fashion is **more/less** important than being practical.

Students of different ages **should/shouldn't** wear the same uniforms.

You look great in your formal clothes! **Move ahead one space.**

Jeans and a sweatshirt **are/aren't** the best clothes for school.

Your clothes aren't very practical. **Go back to start!**

163

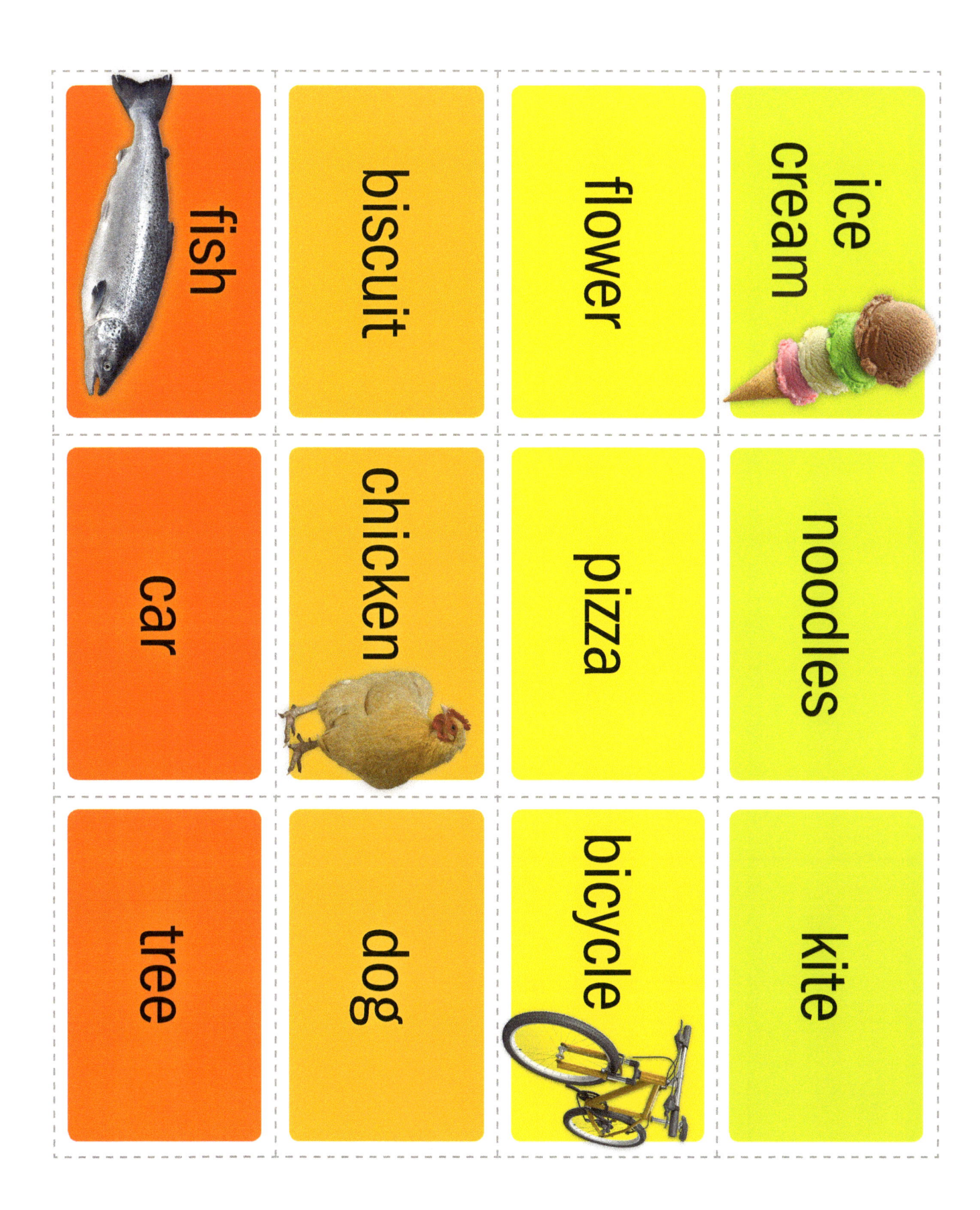

Unit 6 Cutouts Use with Activity 3 on page 97.

fish	biscuit	flower	ice cream
car	chicken	pizza	noodles
tree	dog	bicycle	kite

165

Unit 6 Cutouts Use with Activity 2 on page 104.

Australia
Spain
China
Kenya
Japan
Mexico

fish
vegetables
sweet snacks
tea
rice
meat

167

Unit 7 Cutouts Use with Activity 3 on page 115.

STUDENT A: video game, translator, pen, skateboard, watch

STUDENT B: watch, smartphone, guitar, video game, skateboard

STUDENT C: smartphone, translator, pen, guitar, watch

STUDENT D: pen, watch, video game, translator, guitar

169

Unit 7 Cutouts Use with Activity 3 on page 122.

START

Apps

Fashion

Your predictions don't come true. GO BACK TO START!

Smart homes

Computers

Cars

Games

Passwords

Internet

Food

Your predictions are amazing. GO AHEAD 2 SQUARES!

Gadgets

FINISH

171

Unit 5 Cutouts Use with Activity 2 on page 88.

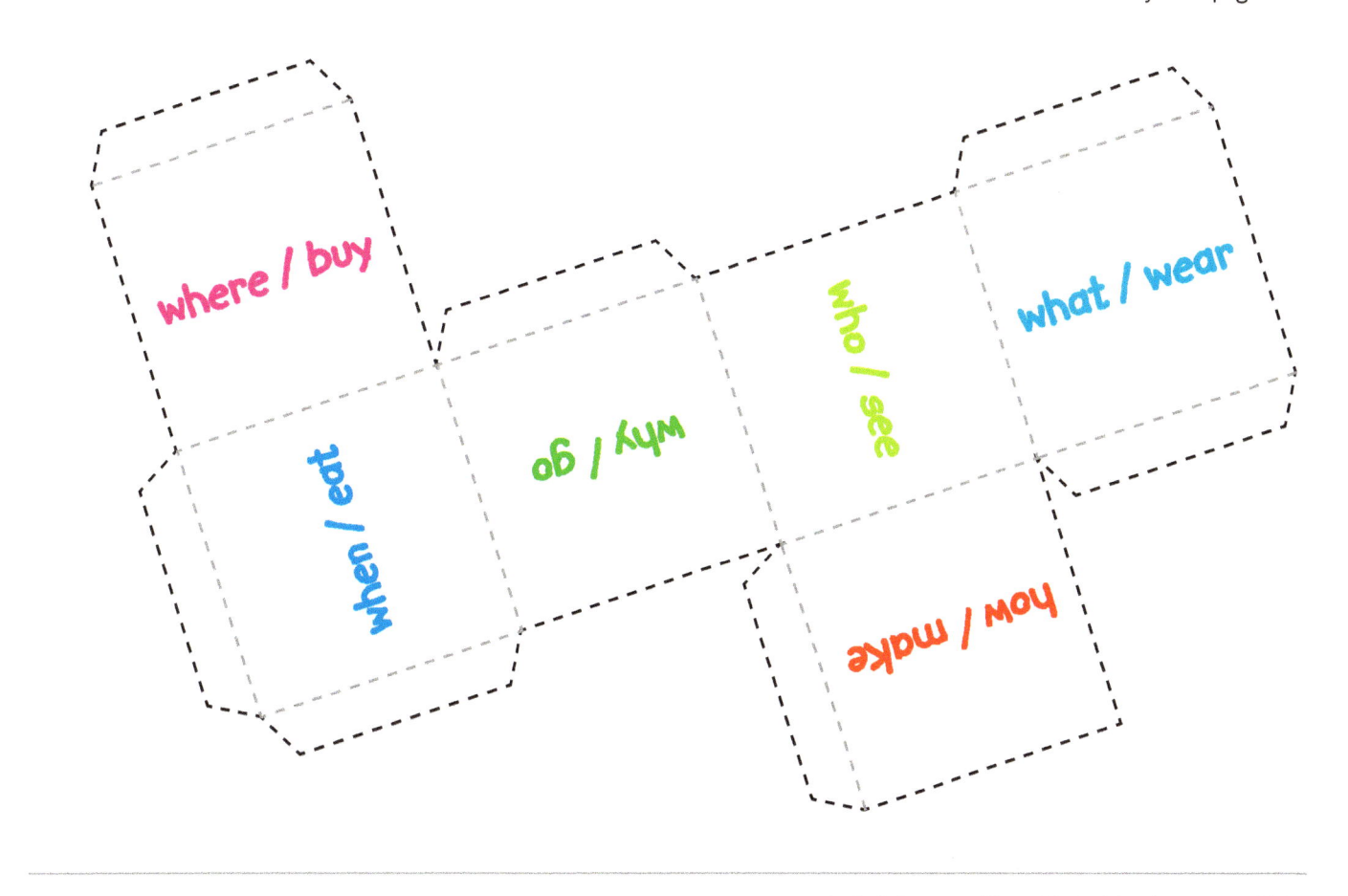

where / buy
when / eat
why / go
who / see
what / wear
how / make

Unit 8 Cutouts Use with Activity 3 on page 131.

I'm really into ...	I don't mind ...	I don't like ... at all.
... is OK, but ... is awful.	**wild**	... is OK.
... is amazing.	... is not bad.	... is awful.

173

Unit 8 Cutouts Use with Activity 3 on page 138.

Will there be …?	There will be …	There aren't …	There is …
Was there …?	There aren't going to be …	There has been …	There are …
Were there …?	Have there been …?	There haven't been …	There isn't …

175

impact
WORKBOOK 1B

SERIES EDITORS
JoAnn (Jodi) Crandall
Joan Kang Shin

Unit 5	What We Wear	46
Unit 6	Mix and Mash	56
	Units 5-6 Review	66
Unit 7	Cool Apps and Gadgets	68
Unit 8	Into the Past	78
	Units 7-8 Review	88
	Choice Activities	94

NATIONAL GEOGRAPHIC
LEARNING

Australia • Brazil • Mexico • Singapore • United Kingdom • United States

Unit 5
What We Wear

1 **Organise the clothes.** Decide if the clothes are practical, formal or casual. Write P, F or C.

2 **Write.** Put words that describe the images in Activity 1 into the puzzle. Then answer the question.

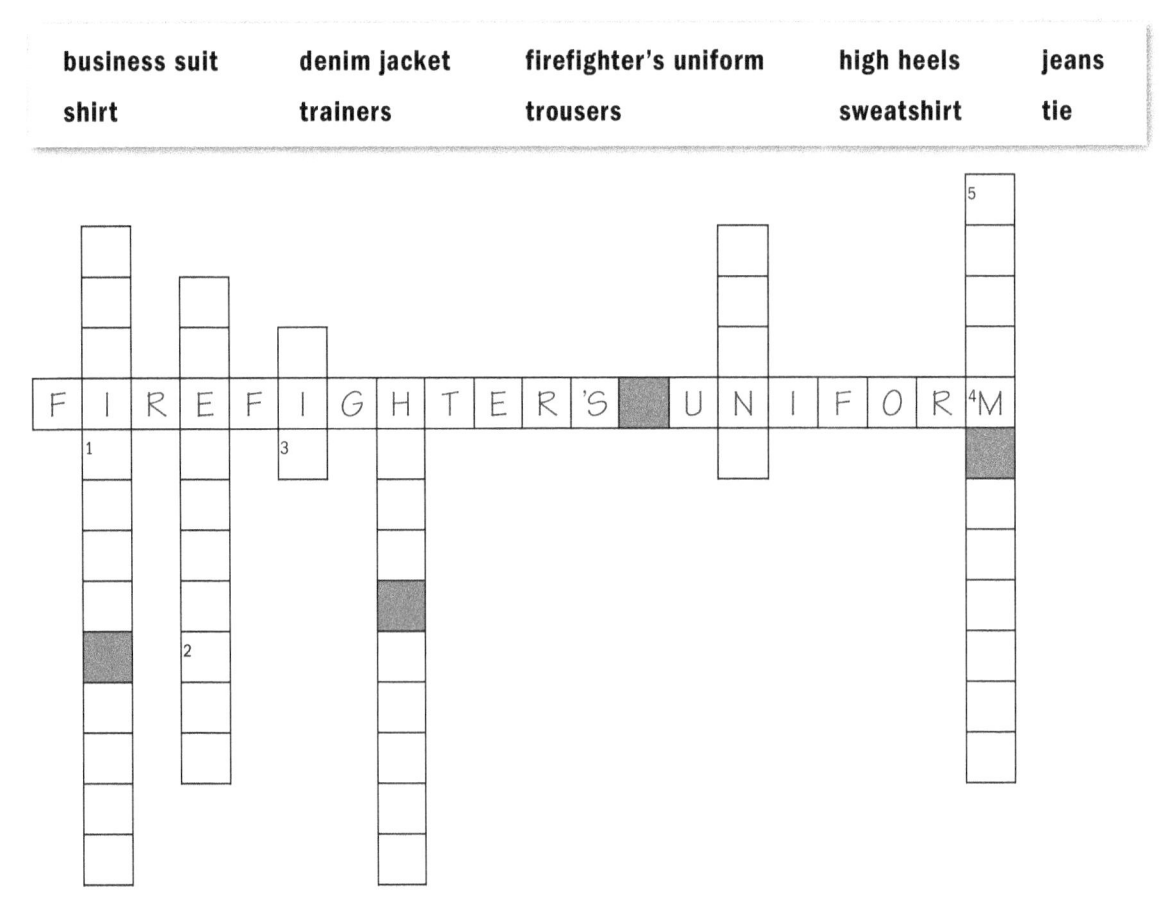

| business suit | denim jacket | firefighter's uniform | high heels | jeans |
| shirt | trainers | trousers | sweatshirt | tie |

F I R E F I G H T E R'S U N I F O R M

Write the letters from the numbered boxes. Then unscramble the letters to find which 19th-century practical fabric is now a 21st-century fashion fabric.

46

3 **Listen.** Complete the student's survey. Then write your answers in the last row. 022

Interviewees	What are you wearing today?	What do you wear at the weekend?
Martin		
Mrs Gardener		
Fiona		
You		

4 **Draw.** Listen to 022 again. Draw the clothes in your notebook. Talk about them in class.

5 **Write.** Survey your friends and classmates. Use words from this unit and your own questions.

Example questions: Do you like to dress up for a party? Which formal clothes do you wear?

| casual | denim | dress up | formal | heels | jeans |
| practical | suit | sweatshirt | tie | tights | uniform |

Interviewees		

47

GRAMMAR

Past simple: Saying what happened

Ami photograph**ed** people in Kenya and India.
They dress**ed** up for the wedding party.
He **didn't dress up** for school.
They **didn't wear** high heels.

Questions:
Did the women paint their hands?
Why **did** they tattoo their faces?

Verbs change when we talk about past events. Most verbs add -ed (protect → protect**ed**)
Be careful with spelling! Verbs ending in e add -d (love → love**d**)
Some verbs double the final letter, then add -ed (stop → sto**pped**)

1 Read. These facts are about the tattoos of Maoris from New Zealand and the Chin people from Myanmar. Are the facts the same (**S**) or different (**D**)? Write **S** or **D**. Then complete the sentences about the Maori and Chin people.

_____ 1. Maori men and women decorated their faces with tattoos. Chin women painted tattoos on their faces.

_____ 2. Maoris used tattoos to show people from other villages or tribes where they lived. Chin women's tattoos showed their village group or tribe.

_____ 3. The government stopped the Chin people putting tattoos on their faces. Maori people didn't stop using tattoos because of the government.

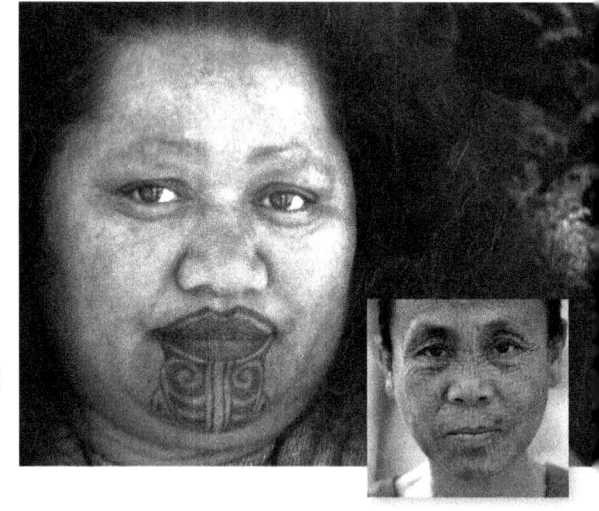

1. In the past, Chin and Maori people both _____

2. Before, Chin women _____

3. The New Zealand government _____

48

2 **Listen.** Draw an arrow. Is the action now or in the past? 🎧 023

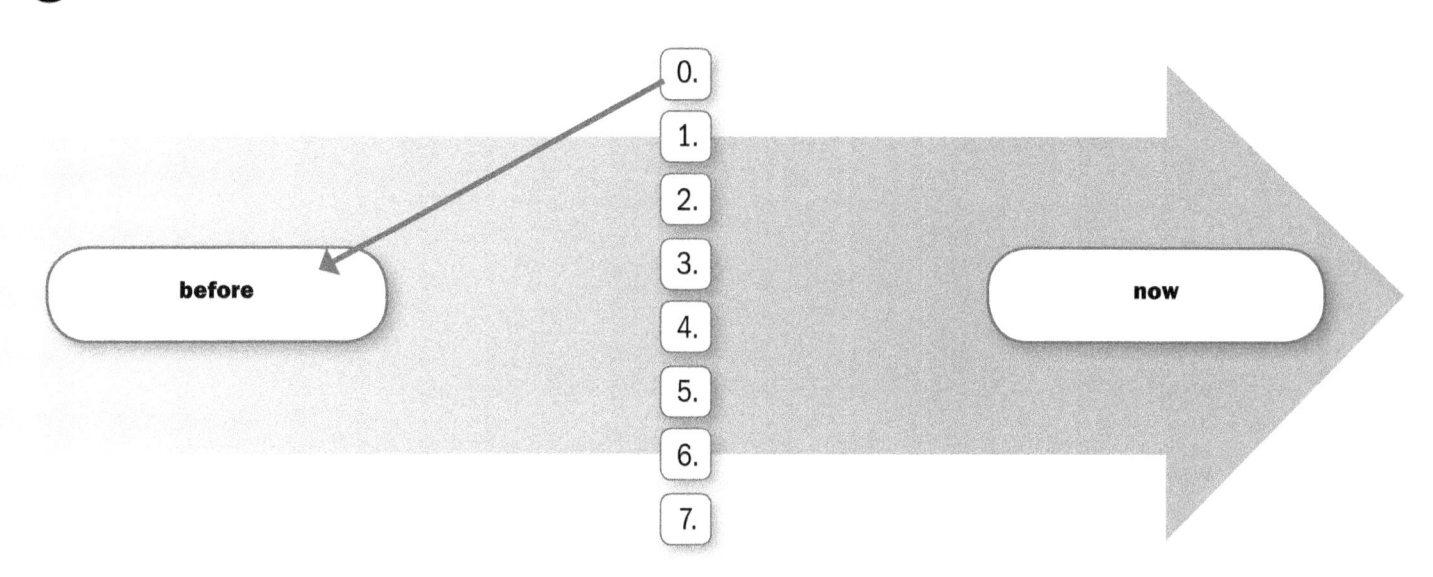

before — 0.
1.
2.
3.
4.
5.
6.
7.
now

3 **Write.** Change the verbs into the past tense to complete the sentences.

1. In the past, Indian mothers (decorate) _____ their daughters' hands and feet.

2. Most Indian brides (pierce) _____ their noses with expensive jewellery.

3. Five thousand years ago, brides (dress up) _____ in bright colours on their wedding days, and this continues today.

4. In the past, many Indian women (collect) _____ over 50 bracelets on one arm, but now they don't wear so many.

5. In the past, Indian men (save) _____ jewellery, but now they save money in the bank.

4 **Write.** Use the words below to write sentences about what people liked to wear in the past. Change the verbs; include some negative verbs. Write one sentence below. Then write four more in your notebooks.

gold jewellery	hair
hazmat suit	high heels
jade bracelets	patterns	tattoos

believe	collect	decorate
like	protect	pull
save	tattoo	use

Many centuries ago, men in India didn't save money in banks. However, they collected gold jewellery.

49

1 **Listen and read.** While you read the article, notice the events in the past and the events in the present. Answer the questions. 024

the History of Jeans

¹ In 1873 two Americans discovered that a cotton fabric called 'jeane' was very strong and practical for outdoor work. Because the fabric came from Nimes (*de Nimes* in French), they called the fabric *denim*. It all started when a customer asked a tailor named Jacob W. Davis to make some strong trousers for her husband. Davis bought some denim from Levi Strauss' shop, and he added rivets to make the pockets strong. The happy husband showed his friends.

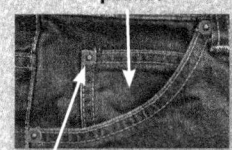

² Davis and Strauss quickly sold 200 more pairs of jeans, but they didn't want other people to copy their idea. So they registered their new product with the government right away, and 20th May, 1873, became the birthday of blue jeans.

³ Today there are many products made of denim, such as bags, boots and ties. Even jewellery such as bracelets, necklaces and hair decorations can be made from denim. Some designers re-use old jeans to create new fashion products, too.

⁴ In the 1800s, or just over a century ago, denim was almost a uniform for outdoor workers. Most people wore it. Today you can spend a lot of money on a denim designer outfit or show your wealth by wearing a diamond accessory on your jeans pocket. But if you haven't got $1,000 to spare, you can still dress up in jeans by wearing high heels.

⁵ Look around you. How many people can you see wearing jeans? There must be a good reason! Maybe it's because jeans are made of a very practical fabric.

1. What did the customer ask the tailor Jacob W. Davis to make? _____

2. How many pairs of trousers did Davis and Strauss sell quickly? _____

3. Name three products made of denim. _____

4. What accessory can you wear on the pocket of your jeans? _____

5. What does the writer believe is the reason for the success of jeans?
_____

2 **Read again.** Find verbs in the past simple tense. Write the events they describe under **In the past**. Write present-day actions in the **Now** column.

In the past	Now

3 **Read the summary.** Write the words from the box in the blanks. Practise telling a classmate or teacher about the history of jeans.

| added | denim | fabric | jeans | practical | wanted |

'Jeane' was a strong, cotton (1) _____ sold in America 200 years ago.

A woman (2) _____ new trousers for her husband.

Jacob Davis bought some (3) _____ from Levi Strauss.

He (4) _____ rivets to make the pockets strong.

Many workers liked the jeans because they were (5) _____.

Davis and Strauss registered their new trousers in 1873 so that nobody could copy their (6) _____.

4 **Read again.** You have read about the history of football uniforms and jeans. Make new sentences about how your clothes have changed over time. Use verbs in the past simple.

_____

_____

_____

51

GRAMMAR

Past simple: Describing what happened

You **were** in the clothes shop. I **was** in the shoe shop. He **had** a denim jacket in his hand. They **put** their mobile phones in their pockets. I **began** jewellery classes last year.	She **kept** extra tights in her bag. We **left** our jackets at the door. He **got** a tie as a birthday present. Shops **sold** thousands of pairs of jeans. I **brought** your sweatshirt for you.

Questions

To form questions with be:
Were you in the clothes shop this morning? **Was** she in the shoe shop?

All other verbs begin with did/didn't:
Didn't you **see** the fashion show? **Did** they **do** exercises to keep healthy?

Some verbs in the past simple do not add *-ed*. They are irregular verbs: *be, begin, bring, buy, do, eat, get, give, have, keep, leave, make, mean, put, see, sell, think, wear*. These past-tense verbs are used often. We must memorise them!

These verbs don't change forms in the past simple: *I (you/he/she/it/we/you/they)* **wore** *new shoes*.

The verb *be* changes when used in the past simple: *I* **was** *(you* **were***, he/she/it* **was***, we/you/they* **were***) in the shoe shop*.

1 **Write.** Look at the photos. Write the verbs in the middle column to complete the sentences.

| became | bought | meant | sold | was | were | wore |

Ski fashion		different in the past.
The clothes		thick and loose.
People		wool and cotton trousers and jackets.
In the 1970s new fabric		available.
Shops		lightweight jackets.
Advanced technology		that fabric changed.
Skiers		colourful all-in-one suits.

2 **Listen.** Circle the correct past simple verb. 🎧 025

1. **thought** / **bought**
2. **was** / **had**
3. **was** / **were**
4. **got** / **put**
5. **sold** / **got**
6. **gave** / **had**

3 **Read the interview.** Write similar questions to interview an older person you know. Show your survey questions in class. If possible, ask your interview questions.

Interviewer:	*Good morning, Mr Daniels. Thank you for speaking to us today.*
Mr Daniels:	*No problem. How can I help?*
Interviewer:	*Could you tell us about how school clothes were different when you were a boy?*
Mr Daniels:	*Oh, well, in my school the uniform was very formal. We wore short, heavy wool trousers. I had a hat and tie, too.*

Question *When did you buy your first pair of jeans?*

Answer _____

Question _____

Answer _____

Question _____

Answer _____

Question _____

Answer _____

Question _____

Answer _____

WRITING

The last stage in writing is publishing. When you publish your work, you let other people read it. But first, you need to make sure it is as good as it can be. You know how to write, review and proofread your work. Do one last check before you show a classmate or teacher.

1 Organise.

1. Your task is to write an essay about a uniform that has changed over time. Think about different types of uniforms, how they are used now, and how they were used in the past. Decide on one type of uniform to research. List changes in clothes, styles, materials and decorations.
2. Plan your ideas. Decide who your readers are. Decide where to publish your paragraph.

Uniform	
Before	
Now	
My readers	
Place for publishing	
Topic sentence	

2 Write.

1. Go to page 89 in your book. Re-read the history of football uniforms.

2. In your notebook, write the first draft of your paragraph about how a uniform has changed over time. Proofread your work. Check your past simple verbs.

3. Write your final draft. Check it one last time, and publish it for your readers.

Now I can ...

- **talk about fashion changes through history.**

    ☐ Yes, I can!
    ☐ I think I can.
    ☐ I need more practice.

    Write about how some clothes have changed over time. Write four sentences.

    1. In the past, _____
    2. Now, _____
    3. In the past, _____
    4. Now, _____

- **use regular past simple verbs.**

    ☐ Yes, I can!
    ☐ I think I can.
    ☐ I need more practice.

    Write sentences using the past tense of some of these words.

    | attach | colour | decorate | dress up | look | mix | pierce | prefer | protect | use |

    1. _____
    2. _____
    3. _____

- **use irregular past simple verbs.**

    ☐ Yes, I can!
    ☐ I think I can.
    ☐ I need more practice.

    Choose words from the box to write sentences using the past tense.

    | begin | bring | buy | eat | get | give | keep | leave | put | see | sell | think |

    1. _____
    2. _____
    3. _____

- **write and share my description of clothes that changed over time.**

    ☐ Yes, I can!
    ☐ I think I can.
    ☐ I need more practice.

    Write two sentences about your personal fashion changes. Share your description with a classmate or teacher.

    _____
    _____

YOU DECIDE Choose an activity. Go to page 94.

Unit 6
Mix and Mash

1 **Find the new vocabulary words.** Look again at pages 94–96 in your book. Find a word that begins with each letter. X = no word.

A _____ B bands C _____ D _____

E _____ F _____ G Gokh-Bi System

H _____ I _____ J Japanese K -X- L -X-

M _____ N no O _____ P _____

Q -X- R _____ S _____ T _____

U urban V _____ W West Africa

X -X- Y you Z -X-

2 **Write.** Cross out the word that doesn't connect to the people. Then choose from the remaining words to complete the sentences. Circle the letter – is it picture A, B or C?

A. DJ
electronic, mix,
song, traditional

B. Band
electronic, traditional,
hit, perform

C. Filmmaker
mix, edit,
recording, video

1. This DJ can _____ two songs together to make a new electronic sound. **A B C**

2. This person works in cities. Her urban _____ stories are cool! **A B C**

3. This is a _____ band. They use natural materials to make their instruments. **A B C**

56

3 **Listen.** Answer the questions. 🎧 026

1. What type of radio show is it? _____

2. The DJ asks three questions. Put them in order. Write 1, 2 and 3.

   a. Whose DJ mix wins the top position? ____

   b. What is the top hit this week? ____

   c. Which song did listeners choose as the top recording? ____

3. Who does the DJ interview? _____

4. Why does he interview her? _____

5. How did she start her music career? _____

6. Do you like electronic music? Why or why not? _____

_____

4 **Draw and write.** Complete the storyboard for a video. Look at the beginning and then draw your ideas for the middle and the end. Use words from the word bank. Tell a classmate about your video.

edit	electronic	fan	hit
hybrid	imitate	include	mix
more	newer	original	perform
popular	record	song	traditional

This traditional band imitates sounds from the forests in Gabon.

GRAMMAR

Adjectives: Comparing two or more things

The band didn't perform their **older** hits.	It's **more difficult** to buy tickets this year.
The light show was **as cool as** last year.	Modern dance is **less tiring than** traditional dance.
The fans are **noisier** tonight than last week!	In my opinion, CDs are **better than** downloads.
The song from the film *Spectre* was a **bigger** hit than other Bond film songs.	The sound quality is **worse** with downloads.

We use comparatives to compare two things. Use *more* before adjectives that have two or more syllables. Add *-er* to adjectives that have just one syllable. With two-syllable adjectives that end in *y*, both options are possible (***more** noisy* or *nois**ier***). Remember to change *y* to *i* before adding *-er*.

Some adjectives have irregular comparative forms: *good* → **better**; *bad* → **worse**

We use *as ... as ...* to describe how things are similar or the same.

1 **Complete the conversation.** Think of the opposites of the words in bold and compare the two things.

Gustav: These new hybrid sports are not **bad**. What do you think? I know you can't play many sports, so which one is (1) _____better_____ for you?

Katia: Disc golf isn't **difficult**, is it? I think it's a little (2) _____ than traditional golf. Do you agree?

Gustav: Sure. It uses **soft** plastic discs, not balls. Those plastic discs are not as (3) _____ as golf balls when you make a mistake!

Katia: Also there aren't any **heavy** golf clubs. Discs are (4) _____ .

Gustav: That's true. And disc golf is **cheap**. My parents say that their golf membership is (5) _____ every year!

Katia: But isn't golf **boring**? Let's try something (6) _____ ! What do you think of volcano boarding?

58

2 **Read.** Find the differences in the musician's notes about two recordings. Change the words in the box to finish the sentences.

Version 1: 12/11/2016
Track 1: Drums – volume high
Bass guitar – comes in too late.
Piano OK – but slow in the middle.
Guitar – OK

Version 2: 17/11/2016
Track 1: Drums – volume low
Bass guitar – much better now.
Piano – love it!
Guitar – can't hear it!

| early | fast | loud | old | quiet |

1. Version 1, from 12th November, is _____ than Version 2.

2. The drums on Version 1 are _____ than the drums on Version 2.

3. In Version 2, the bass guitar comes in _____ than in Version 1.

4. The piano is _____ in the middle of Version 2.

5. In Version 2, the guitar is _____ .

3 **Listen.** Which picture is the speaker describing, in your opinion? Circle A or B. Then complete the sentences. 027

1. I love these hybrid lamps! Lamp A / B is (cool) _____ than lamp A / B because _____.

2. I think lamp A / B is (useful) _____ than lamp A / B because _____.

3. Which version is good? Lamp A / B is (good/bad) _____ than lamp A / B because _____.

4. Lamp A / B is (bright) _____ than lamp A / B because _____.

59

1 **Listen and read.** While you read, notice the differences between the traditional and the modern activities. 🎧 028

Skipping Filipino Style

1. Mix the past with the present and you get a traditional dance from the Philippines plus a cool new type of sports activity! Tinikling is a fun form of exercise that combines rhythm with fast foot- and legwork. The original sport began in central Philippines and imitates the tikling bird walking carefully through grass and bamboo. Tinikling improves awareness of space and includes skills similar to skipping. Every year young people perform it in school shows all over the Philippines, and audiences love it.

2. Tinikling is a type of dance that involves two people hitting bamboo poles together and on the ground. This makes the beat or rhythm. At the same time, one or more dancers step over and in between the poles. It's not easy, especially for girls who wear long traditional dresses! In the traditional dance, bamboo poles make the beat along with music from a type of string instrument. Today's 21st century version uses simpler, four-beat electronic dance music.

3. There are many tinikling products available now, such as tinikling songs on CDs and audio downloads, dance-step instruction videos, and tinikling sticks made of bamboo or plastic. For the traditional version, you must find thick bamboo poles, but be careful – just imagine the pain if you make a mistake!

2 **Read the article again.** Answer the questions.

1. What activity is tinikling similar to?

   _____

2. What are the dancers and the bamboo poles imitating?

   _____

3. What modern-day products can we buy for tinikling?

   _____

3 **Re-read the article.** Compare the differences and similarities between the traditional dance and the sport of today. Practise telling a classmate or your teacher about tinikling.

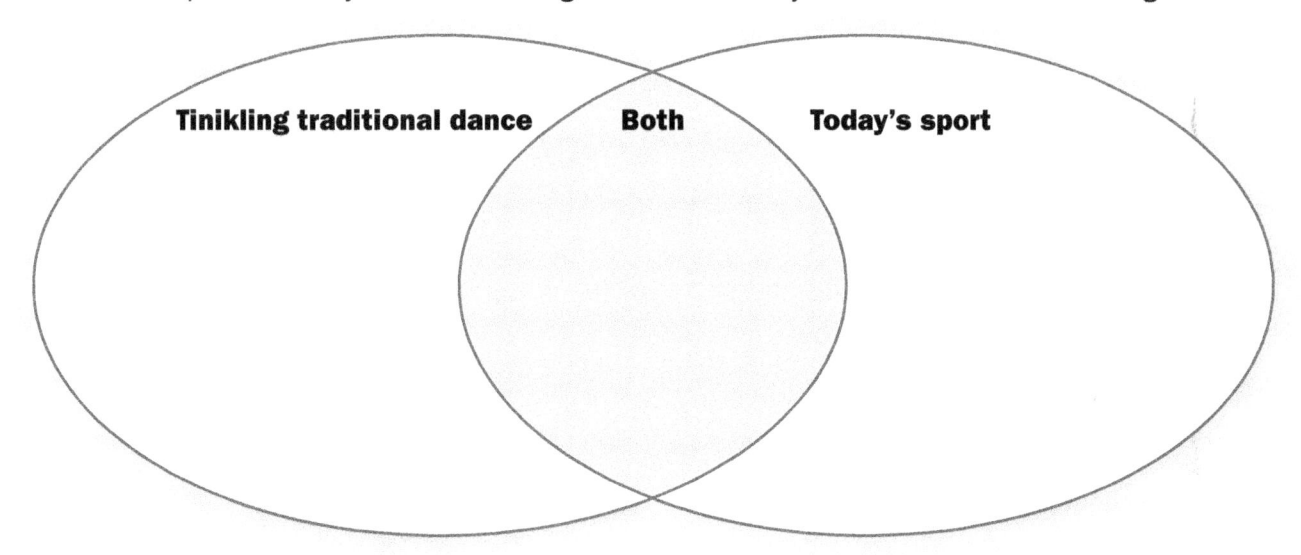

Tinikling traditional dance | **Both** | **Today's sport**

4 **Write.** Read the text again. Write two new sentences about changes in this traditional dance.

Example: The traditional music for the dance was more complex than today's four-beat rhythm.

_____

_____

_____

_____

61

GRAMMAR

Countable and uncountable nouns: Talking about amounts

Countable nouns	Uncountable nouns
Many / Some / A lot of / A few cultures have a traditional dance. They perform **a few** traditional songs. She saw **a couple of** shows last month.	**Some / A little / A lot of /** modern dance mixes words, too. Listening to **a little** music before the show is a good idea. There is **too much** information on fan websites.
Questions How **many** downloads were there? Were there **many** fans outside the door?	**Questions** How **much** money do we need? Did they make **much** noise?

Countable nouns are nouns we can count (*one song, two songs*). Uncountable nouns are nouns we can't count (*music, time*). They don't have a plural form. We can't use *a/an* or numbers before uncountable nouns. Use *a few/many* to talk about countable nouns and *a little/much* to talk about uncountable nouns.

1 **Read.** Look at the nouns in **bold** and circle *UC* (uncountable nouns) or *C* (countable nouns).

1. Hiro is planning his birthday meal, so he's checking how much **food** he has ready. (UC / C)

2. Is there enough **juice**? (UC / C)

3. Hiro needs to buy two or three more **bottles** of juice. (UC / C)

4. He wants to share a birthday **pizza**. A sushi-pizza! (UC / C)

5. Eight people need some **pizza**. (UC / C)

6. Everyone will probably eat at least one **piece** of sushi-pizza. (UC / C)

7. Hiro only bought two **boxes** of sushi-pizza. (UC / C)

8. His friends all love sushi-pizza. Hiro has to buy more **pizza**. (UC / C)

2 **Write.** Look at this menu. Sort the food in **bold** into countable and uncountable nouns.

Viva Tacos! Traditional Mexican flour and corn tortillas

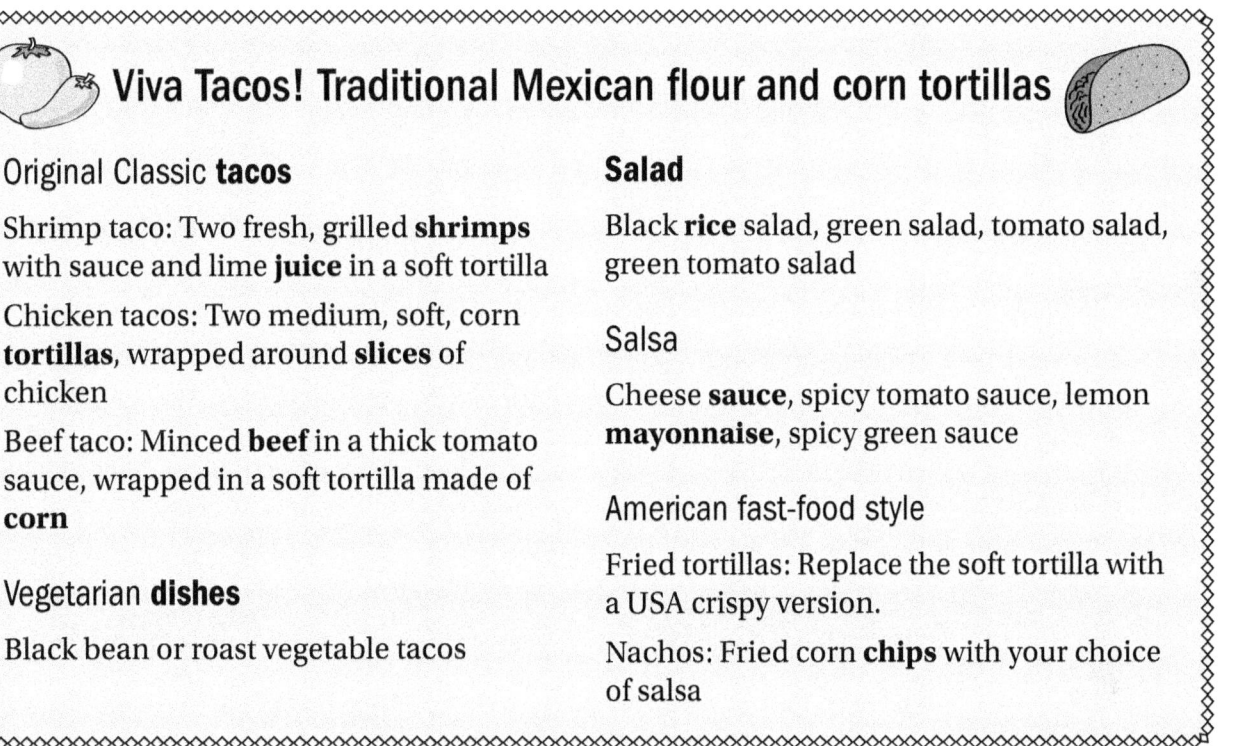

Original Classic tacos

Shrimp taco: Two fresh, grilled **shrimps** with sauce and lime **juice** in a soft tortilla

Chicken tacos: Two medium, soft, corn **tortillas**, wrapped around **slices** of chicken

Beef taco: Minced **beef** in a thick tomato sauce, wrapped in a soft tortilla made of **corn**

Vegetarian **dishes**

Black bean or roast vegetable tacos

Salad

Black **rice** salad, green salad, tomato salad, green tomato salad

Salsa

Cheese **sauce**, spicy tomato sauce, lemon **mayonnaise**, spicy green sauce

American fast-food style

Fried tortillas: Replace the soft tortilla with a USA crispy version.

Nachos: Fried corn **chips** with your choice of salsa

Countable nouns	Uncountable nouns

3 **Listen.** What do the friends choose to eat? 029

Choice 1: _____

Choice 2: _____

Choice 3: _____

4 **Write.** Read the menu again. Write questions about some of the food in the box.

| black rice | chicken slices | lemon mayonnaise |
| roast vegetable tacos | spicy tomato sauce | corn tortillas |

How many: _____

How much: _____

Are there: _____

Is there: _____

63

WRITING

A good paragraph of exemplification introduces your idea and uses examples to support that idea. We use *for example*, *another example* and *such as* to introduce these supporting sentences.

1 Organise.

1. Your task is to write a paragraph about your own unique ani-mix. Think of two or more animals and mix them together. Draw your animal in your notebook. You need to imagine its name and write examples of how it is unique.

2. Plan your ideas in the table. Research your chosen animals, their appearance and what they can do. If possible, create a photo of your chosen ani-mix to go with your paragraph.

	Animal 1	Animal 2	Animal 3
Name			
Size and appearance			
Body parts (legs, wings)			
Abilities (climbs, swims)			

2 Write.

1. Go to page 105 in your book. Re-read the model and writing prompt.

2. Write your first draft. Check for organisation, content, punctuation, capitalisation and spelling.

3. Write your final draft. Share it with your teacher and classmates.

Now I can ...

- **talk about how two things combine to make something new.**

    Write three sentences about how artists combine ideas.

    1. _____
    2. _____
    3. _____

    ☐ Yes, I can!
    ☐ I think I can.
    ☐ I need more practice.

- **compare two or more things.**

    Complete the sentences using the given words.

    1. Tinikling is _____ (cool) than skipping.

    2. Mash-up music is _____ (difficult) to perform than many people think.

    3. I think cooking fried rice is _____ (easy) than baking cakes.

    ☐ Yes, I can!
    ☐ I think I can.
    ☐ I need more practice.

- **use countable and uncountable nouns.**

    Write sentences using these words.   food   meat   songs   videos

    1. _____
    2. _____
    3. _____
    4. _____

    ☐ Yes, I can!
    ☐ I think I can.
    ☐ I need more practice.

- **write a paragraph of exemplification.**

    Write about your idea for a new mix of art, sports or music. Support your idea with examples. Plan and check your paragraph. Present it to your classmates and teacher.

    ☐ Yes, I can!
    ☐ I think I can.
    ☐ I need more practice.

    _____
    _____
    _____

YOU DECIDE Choose an activity. Go to page 95.

Units 5–6 Review

1 Read. Choose the correct word to complete the sentences.

1. Wei doesn't like formal clothes.

    He takes off his school ____ as soon as he gets home.
    a. uniform **b.** jeans **c.** tights

2. The DJ preferred the second version of the song.

    He thought the newer mix was ____ than the first one.
    a. worse **b.** better **c.** noisier

3. I like to include stars in all my paintings.

    I ____ stars into all my art work.
    a. mix **b.** perform **c.** record

4. What type of ____ was the singer wearing on her arms and wrists?
    a. necklace **b.** tie **c.** bracelet

5. My mother works in a laboratory.

    She has to wear a special suit, for ____ reasons.
    a. practical **b.** formal **c.** casual

6. Video game designers have to be more creative every year. They have to

    ____ cool, new ideas that nobody has tried.
    a. combine **b.** imitate **c.** imagine

2 Listen. Decide if the sentences are *True* (T) or *False* (F). 030

1. The original recording was from the 1980s. ____

2. He doesn't like formal clothes. ____

3. She thinks her friend looks good. ____

4. The girl asks for her mother's opinion about her hair. ____

5. The boy prefers traditional guitar music. ____

3 Read. Choose the best answer to the questions.

1. The wimple was a popular head covering for women in Europe from the 12th to the 15th century. Wimples were usually made of cotton or silk. They provided protection from the weather, and they were a way to dress up for formal occasions. Sometimes the wimple covered the top of the head and shoulders, and went around the neck, finishing up at the chin.

2. Wealthy women sometimes used the wimple to display their jewellery. They decorated the cloth before placing it on their head. Sometimes a circle of fabric or metal, like a queen's crown, was placed on the head to hold the wimple in place.

3. Head covering is an ancient fashion for both women and men. Many centuries ago, men and women in Ancient Greece, Rome and China covered their heads for a variety of reasons. Today people from countries around the Mediterranean still wear similar coverings to protect them from the strong sun and to dress up on formal occasions.

1. What was the wimple made from?
   a. wool   **b.** denim   **c.** cotton

2. For how many centuries was the wimple in fashion in Europe?
   a. six   **b.** four   **c.** one

3. Which part of the body did the wimple not cover?
   a. shoulders   **b.** hands   **c.** neck

4. What did some women add to their wimple to show their wealth?
   a. jewellery   **b.** paint   **c.** flowers

4 Read the sentences. Circle the correct word.

1. My sweatshirt looks cleaner than yours because I **wash** / **washed** it last week.

2. **Some** / **Much** brides in Morocco still **paint** / **painted** their hands, and in this way they keep the tradition alive.

3. **Many** / **Much** Indian women **pierce** / **pierced** their noses when they got married.

4. Today **a few** / **a little** young Maoris still **wear** / **wore** tattoos on their faces.

5. When she was a teenager, my mum **loves** / **loved** hybrid songs.

6. Last year my neighbour **hates** / **hated** my favourite type of music, but now she likes **much** / **many** of it!

Unit 7
Cool Apps and Gadgets

1 **Write.** Find four vocabulary words or phrases from this unit on the screen. Then use them to complete the text message.

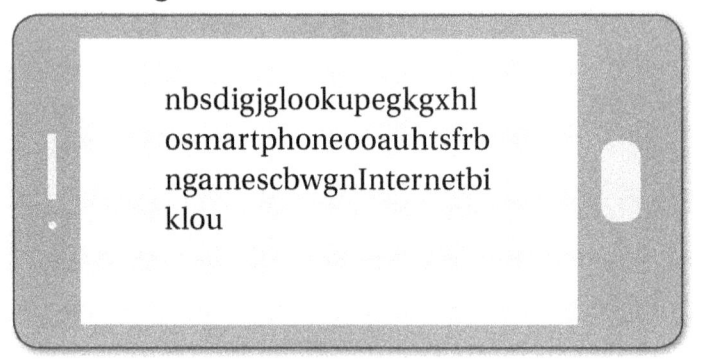

```
nbsdigjglookupegkgxhl
osmartphoneooauhtsfrb
ngamescbwgnInternetbi
klou
```

Can you please _____

2 **Write.** Use words from the word bank to send a message. Write on the smartphone.

apps	chat	connect	incredible	mobile	possible	search
send	share	tablet	text	useful	Wi-Fi	

3 **Read.** Match the words with the definitions. Write the letter on the line.

____ 1. chat　　　　　　a. to allow another person to use something too

____ 2. share　　　　　 b. able to move from place to place

____ 3. mobile　　　　 c. to join two things together

____ 4. connect　　　　d. about computer technology

____ 5. digital　　　　 e. to talk

4 **Listen.** Match each speaker to his or her words. Write the name on the line. 🎧031

1. _____

> I love using mobile apps to chat with my friends.

2. _____

> It's easier to send a text than to walk upstairs to my room, says my mum!

3. _____

> Sorry, I need help with my photo-sharing app.

4. _____

> Share my gadget webpage!

5 **Complete the responses.** Use words from the box and your own ideas.

| gadgets | Internet | look up | share | smartphone | useful |

1. I'll send everybody the coolest photo from the party – this is my favourite!

   Please don't _____

2. I'll send a text when I get on the train. It's the easiest way to talk to you.

   Did you _____

3. My brother's going to ask for a tablet as a birthday present. He needs to search the Internet and wants to play games, but a basic version is OK.

   Lucky him! For my next birthday, _____

4. Are you going to finish your electricity project before Friday? I'm not! Can you please send me some useful images?

   We need to search for _____

69

GRAMMAR

Superlatives: Talking about extremes

The scariest part of the film is at the beginning.
This dictionary app is **the most useful** one I have.
This game scores **the highest** in this year's reviews, but it's my least favourite.
That café on the corner has **the worst** Wi-Fi connection in town.

We use superlatives to compare one thing in a group to the rest of the group. Superlatives always take *the*.
Use *most* before adjectives that have two or more syllables:
*It's **the most difficult** computer game.*
Add *–est* to adjectives that have just one syllable:
*This is **the loudest** setting on my mobile phone.*
With two-syllable adjectives that end in *y*, both options are possible: *the scariest* or *the most scary*. (Remember to change *y* to *i*.)
Use *least* with any adjective: *the **least** difficult, the **least** scary, the **least** loud.*
Some adjectives have their own superlative form: *good/bad* → **the best/the worst**.

1 **Read.** Circle the correct words. Complete the reviews.

1. This **keyboard / camera / battery** is for French speakers. It's (+/unusual) _____ one I've ever seen.

2. When we watch videos on our smartphones, we use a lot of **battery / camera / keyboard** life. (+/good) _____ one lasts one whole day.

3. The **microphone / camera / keyboard** on this video camera is not (+/powerful) _____ , but it's built-in, so it's easier to transport and you never forget it.

4. We all know that the **keyboard / screen / battery** on a smartphone is easy to break. Today I dropped (+/ expensive) _____ phone I've ever had and broke it!

2 **Listen.** While you listen, read the questions. Listen again and circle the letters. 032

1. Which camera is the least expensive? A B C D
2. Which camera has the smallest screen? A B C D
3. Which product has the worst zoom? A B C D
4. Which is the heaviest? A B C D
5. Which is the most expensive to buy? A B C D

3 **Write.** Match the opposites. Then change the pairs to their superlatives. Choose one word from the pair to complete the statements.

easy good high loud	bad difficult low quiet
_____ easiest _____	_____ most difficult _____
_____	_____
_____	_____
_____	_____

1. I finished in two minutes! This computer game puzzle is _____ we have tried this term.

2. You're amazing! Your score is _____ ever!

3. Which smartphone has _____ volume control?

4. My old phone had _____ screen quality! I couldn't see any texts at night!

5. That free download app is _____ I have ever tried – I can't get past level one!

4 **Read the e-mail.** Write a reply.

> Hi!
> I'm doing a survey about computer games, websites and apps. Can you please take a moment to answer these questions?
> What are the best / worst / funniest / most useful / least exciting computer games, websites and apps that you know? Please explain why.
> Thank you!
> JJ

_____
_____
_____
_____

1 **Listen and read.** As you read, notice the main idea and the details. 🎧 033

Mobile Magic!

¹ What connects government offices in Nigeria, doctors in Malawi and farmers in El Salvador? The answer is … useful mobile phone software invented by Ken Banks. In Africa, Ken noticed that people in rural areas travelled for hours to share information. Because people there are not connected to the Internet, he decided mobile phones could help.

² All you need is a laptop computer and a mobile phone. It doesn't have to be the newest smartphone. An old or recycled phone is fine. 'After downloading the free software, you never need the Internet again,' Ken explains. Attach your phone to the laptop, type your message on the computer keyboard, select the people you want to contact, and hit 'Send'. The message goes to mobile phones as a text!

³ So what do people send messages about? One good example is in Malawi. Ken sent a hundred recycled phones and a laptop with his software downloaded. After training for two weeks, doctors in the city can communicate with rural villages to decide which medical supplies to bring on their visits. These texts save time and thousands of dollars in travel costs. Even more importantly, a group of doctors in Malawi can now help the highest number of patients ever.

⁴ Ken tells us, 'We need to help people recognise that you can do useful things without lots of money or expensive technology.'

2 **Read.** Answer the questions.

1. Which continent gave Ken the idea to design mobile phone software?
   _____

2. How many times do you need to connect to the Internet to access this service?
   _____

3. Give two examples of how Ken's invention can help people in Africa.
   _____
   _____

3 **Write.** Choose the main idea for each paragraph, and write it in the table. Then complete the table with the details A–F. Write the letters in the spaces.

> How it works   Ken's message   One example   Introduction

A. Type a message on the laptop.
B. Africans travel for hours to share information.
C. Thousands of hours and travel costs are saved, and many more patients are helped.
D. They are not connected to the Internet, but phones might help.
E. Click 'Send' and the message goes to mobile phones in a text.
F. Doctors send messages to mobile phones in rural villages.

	Main idea	Details
Paragraph 1		1. Nigeria, Malawi, El Salvador use Ken's text software. 2. ____ 3. ____
Paragraph 2		1. Connect phone to laptop. 2. ____ 3. ____
Paragraph 3		1. Malawi doctors received 100 phones, 1 laptop and training. 2. ____ 3. ____
Concluding sentence		We don't need a lot of money or technology to be useful.

4 **Think about the information from the reading text.** You've read about a useful text message service. Tick (✓) the sentences that are true.

☐ Only two or three countries can use the text service.

☐ Someone needs to type a message on a laptop.

☐ It saves people a lot of travelling time.

☐ It's only useful for doctors.

☐ Mobile phones can receive text messages.

GRAMMAR

Will and going to: Talking about the future

Schools **will have** chat rooms where students can ask questions online to teachers.	Wi-Fi **is going to speed up** in developing countries.
Smartphones **won't cost** so much money.	The Internet **isn't going to replace** teachers.
Will there **be** more female computer game designers? **Yes**, I think there **will be**.	**Are** our screens **going to affect** our eyesight? We**'re going to need** better eye tests.

To make predictions about the future, we use *will* or *going to*.
Will + verb: *will be, will go, will cost*
present form of *be* + *going to* + verb: *am/is/are* going *to* have
will not = won't
will = 'll

1 **Listen.** Circle the form of the verb that you hear. 🎧 034

1. South Korea **is going to be** / **will be** a world leader in digital technology.

2. India **is going to build** / **will build** many new Wi-Fi towers.

3. Estonia **will continue to be** / **is going to be** very involved in the digital age.

4. Some experts say that many more countries **will enter** / **are going to enter** the race for the best designs in mobile technology.

5. Village farmers **are going to pay for** / **will pay for** services with their smartphones.

6. More people **are going to use** / **will use** taxis because it's easier to order one through the Internet.

2 **Listen.** Tick the pictures that are in the description you hear. 🎧 035

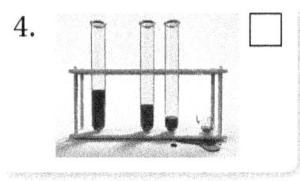

1. ☐ 2. ☐ 3. ☐

4. ☐ 5. ☐ 6. ☐

74

3 Read the blog. Circle the correct answers.

¹ Learning from our own mistakes is useful, but learning from another country's mistakes is going to be the fastest way to develop, I say.

² India has been developing its technology for many years. Other countries may have started before us, but today they often still have old technology – for example, unmodernised telephone systems. We can learn from this. First, we need to look at the original technology. We'll look at the problems but keep the best designs. But then we'll search for the latest ideas, and create something similar but better. Countries like India are catching up. But there's competition! Some experts say that Estonia is going to be the most creative country for gadgets, and India will jump ahead with mobile phone technology.

³ How will India jump in front? For example, now most people in India go shopping in street markets and small, local shops. There aren't any large supermarkets in rural areas, so people have to travel to buy more expensive products. But soon we'll start to buy things using the Internet on our smartphones. We're still going to use our small shops and markets, but we'll 'jump' over the need for supermarkets. Get ready – change will come fast!

1. What does the writer think is going to be the best way to improve her country?
   a. Learning from another country's mistakes
   b. Making mistakes
   c. Copying old technology

2. How will countries like India design new gadgets and technology?
   a. They will keep the same old technology.
   b. They will copy and improve on existing technology.
   c. They won't spend any time on new ideas.

3. According to the blog, which country is going to design the most creative gadgets?
   a. Estonia   b. India   c. Britain

4. How will India 'jump in front' of more developed countries?
   a. India will spend more money on travel.
   b. Indians won't use the Internet.
   c. Indians will use technology to develop smart solutions to everyday problems.

4 Write. Read the text in Activity 3 again. Write about some of the ideas in the text in your own words, using *will* and *going to*.

_____

_____

_____

WRITING

To write a good review of a product, we need descriptive words. We want our readers to imagine the product clearly. Details are important, so remember to list good and bad things about the product, and give examples of each.

1 Organise.

1. Your task is to write a review of a product that you have used. Look through the unit for product ideas, or do some research on the Internet, then think of similar products you have used.

2. Plan your writing. Your review needs examples of good and bad points. Finish with your opinion and the reasons that support it.

Use the table to help you plan. List the examples you will use in your review.

Product	
Good points	
Bad points	
Your opinion and reasons	

2 Write.

1. Go to page 123 in your book. Re-read the model and writing prompt.

2. Write your first draft. Check for organisation, content, punctuation, capitalisation and spelling.

3. Write your final draft. Share it with your teacher and classmates.

Now I can ...

- **talk about cool apps and gadgets.**

  ☐ Yes, I can!
  ☐ I think I can.
  ☐ I need more practice.

  Write two sentences about apps and gadgets. Give examples of what they can do.

  _____

  _____

- **use superlatives to talk about extremes.**

  ☐ Yes, I can!
  ☐ I think I can.
  ☐ I need more practice.

  Complete the conversation with the superlatives.
  Example: Your music app is (+/cool) ___the coolest___ I have seen!

  Pietro: Have you heard (+/new) _____ download from this band?

  Camilla: No! Do you think it's their (+/good) _____ version?

  Pietro: Well, we could look up a review to see (+/high) _____ rated downloads.

  Camilla: OK, but that band is my (-/favourite) _____ . Can we look up this other band as well?

- **talk about the future using *will* and *going to*.**

  ☐ Yes, I can!
  ☐ I think I can.
  ☐ I need more practice.

  Write about the photo using *will* and *going to*.

  _____

  _____

- **write a review.**

  ☐ Yes, I can!
  ☐ I think I can.
  ☐ I need more practice.

  Write about a product. Include examples of its good and bad points, as well as your opinion about the product.

  _____

  _____

  _____

YOU DECIDE Choose an activity. Go to page 96.

Unit 8
Into the Past

1 **Write.** Combine the words in the bones to make a question. Write the question on the first line. Answer the question using two of the words from the word bank. Write your answer on the second line.

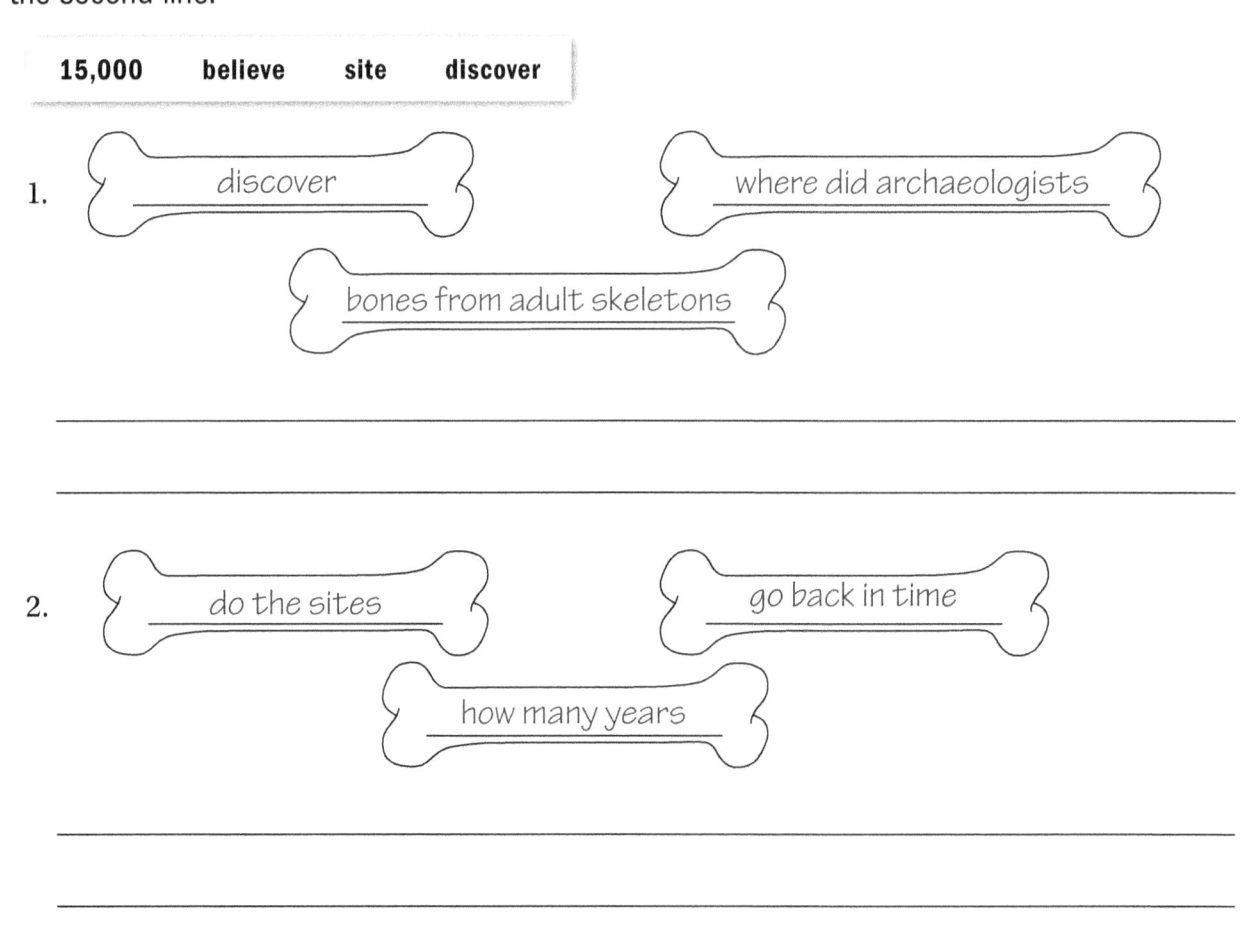

| 15,000 | believe | site | discover |

1. _discover_ / _where did archaeologists_ / _bones from adult skeletons_

   _____

   _____

2. _do the sites_ / _go back in time_ / _how many years_

   _____

   _____

2 **Write.** Match the words and phrases with similar meanings. Then use the words or phrases to complete the sentences.

1. bones   a. ancestors
2. continue to think b. skull
3. origins   c. still believe

Experts put together a human (1) _____ and some skeletal (2) _____ .

Some scientists (3) _____ that the (4) _____ of American people are Asian, but others (5) _____ a different story about their (6) _____ .

3 Listen. Complete the summary using the words in the box. 036

| adult | advanced | ancestors | believe |
| bones | discovered | skeleton | skull |

Scientists _____ that they have _____ the origins of the American people.

The answer came from a nearly complete _____ and _____ found in the sea near Mexico. It belonged to a young woman, almost an _____. Scientists used _____ computers to make a model head from the _____ bones and now think that the common _____ of the first Americans may have come from Asia.

4 Write. Use the words from Activity 3 and the box below to make sentences.

| there + be | has/have + discover/believe |

_____

_____

_____

_____

_____

_____

79

GRAMMAR

Present perfect: Describing a past action that still continues

Chess **has been** popular for hundreds of years.
I **have played** chess for five years.
My brother **hasn't played** board games since he started playing video games.
Have you always **liked** video games? Yes, I **have**.
How long **have** you **played** video games?

We use the present perfect to talk about actions that began in the past but continue in the present.

To form the present perfect, use *have* or *has* and a past participle of the verb. Most verbs form the past participle by adding *-ed*, but some verbs are irregular. (be → been, go → gone)

We use *for* with the present perfect to talk about how long it has been from the moment an action or situation began until the present moment.

For + period of time: **for** two years, **for** five days, **for** a very long time

We use *since* with the present perfect to talk about when an action or situation began.

Since + a point in time: **since** last week, **since** 2015, **since** I arrived

1 **Complete the sentences.** Write the correct form of the verb in brackets and select *for* or *since*.

1. My father _____ (play) chess _____ (for / since) 40 years.

2. My two brothers _____ (play) chess _____ (for / since) they were little, too.

3. I _____ (play) chess _____ (for / since) just one year, but it _____ (become) my favourite game!

4. My father _____ never _____ (like) video games, but my mother _____ always _____ (love) them.

5. I've never liked video games, but that _____ (change) _____ (for / since) last week. I _____ (discover) a really cool video game about ancient Rome.

6. I only started to play a week ago, but I _____ (complete) all levels!

80

2 Listen. Circle the sentence with the present perfect form. 🎧 037

1.
   a. They discovered bones in a cave.
   b. They've drawn a map showing the bones in the cave.
   c. They show the map of the cave to the newspapers.

2.
   a. Scientists have studied early civilisations similar to our ancestors.
   b. Scientists believe that modern humans are less healthy.
   c. Our ancestors slept better than us.

3.
   a. Rajiv moved his queen three squares closer to Amena's king.
   b. Amena hasn't forgotten that the queen is a powerful chess piece.
   c. Amena blocks Rajiv's queen with another piece.

3 Listen again. Complete the sentences with the present perfect form of the verb. 🎧 037

1. First, they found bones in the cave. Next, they drew a map of the cave to show the newspapers. The journalists (see) _____ the map now.

2. Our ancestors slept very well. Modern humans don't sleep very well. Scientists (find) _____ that early civilisations can help us understand our sleep problems.

3. Rajiv moved his queen closer to Amena's king. Amena knows that the queen is a powerful chess piece. Rajiv (not win) _____ the chess game yet.

4 Write. Use the words to make sentences using the present perfect.

1. Experts are looking for descendants of the last King of India. They / find / some descendants / in Myanmar and Pakistan / but / most / live / India all their lives.

   _____

2. Archaeologists in Russia / discover / unusually long skulls / site named Arkaim.

   _____

81

1 Listen and read. As you read, think about what scientists have learnt about ancient civilisations. 🎧038

My History Page

Wait – change the history books!
Which is the oldest civilisation in Southeast Asia?

¹ For many years, scientists have thought that the oldest human civilisation in Southeast Asia was from India, because humans have lived there for at least 10,000 years. Scientists believed that those early people moved east, and that their descendants populated other countries, such as my country, Sri Lanka. So this is what our education system has always taught teenagers like me.

² But new technology shows that there has been civilisation in ancient Sri Lanka for much longer, dating back 30,000 years. Since the 1980s, archaeologists have studied skeletons that show cultures have survived almost three times longer than we previously believed. Finger bones and skulls discovered in archaeological sites in dry caves show that the ancestors of modern Sri Lankans were advanced enough to make their homes in caves 30,000 years ago. That's 20,000 years before people in Europe did this!

³ So Sri Lankans now have new information about our origins. We have learnt that our ancestors were almost the first humans to use tools to cut stone and hunt animals. I say 'almost the first' because Sri Lankans are not the oldest civilisation in the world. That prize goes to South Africa, where people have lived for an amazing 50,000 years! As technology improves, scientists must keep looking to see if they really have discovered the oldest sites in your country, too.

2 Read again. Answer the questions.

1. Which country did experts think had the oldest human civilisation in Southeast Asia?
   _____

2. How many years have civilisations lived in Sri Lanka? _____

3. What were the ancient Sri Lankans doing 20,000 years before the Europeans?
   _____

4. Which country has the oldest civilisation in the world? _____

82

3 Read. Match the cause with the effect. Write the number on the line.

Cause

1. Experts thought that India was the oldest civilisation in Southeast Asia.

2. Scientists discovered bones from 30,000 years ago in Sri Lanka.

3. Scientists used modern technology to find the age of the bones.

Effect

_____ Now, there are plans to search for older sites in other countries, too.

_____ So, schools taught that Sri Lankans were descendants of Indians.

_____ So, now we know there have been Sri Lankan civilisations for much longer.

4 Write. Read the text again. Write the cause and three possible effects in the graphic organiser. Write the letters in the spaces.

A. Archaeologists might search for older sites in other countries, too.

B. Scientists discovered 30,000-year-old bones in Sri Lanka.

C. Sri Lankan school books may need rewriting!

D. Europeans have learnt that their ancestors are younger than Sri Lankans' ancestors.

5 Write. In this unit, you have read about the origins of civilisations and the changing lives of young people. Write possible effects for these causes.

1. Cause: The Aztec education system taught boys and girls separate subjects.

   Effect: _____

2. Cause: Archaeologists don't always use the most modern technology in every country.

   Effect: _____

3. Cause: Many centuries ago, most adults could not read or write.

   Effect: _____

4. Cause: Some poor teenagers worked in factories in England in the 1800s.

   Effect: _____

83

GRAMMAR

There + to be: Expressing existence at different points of time

There was going to be a talk about teenage art and culture tonight.	But unfortunately, **there isn't** anybody available to speak at the moment.
In any teenager's life **there are** always good times and bad times.	**Were there** difficult times for you, too? Yes, **there've been** many!
At the camp **there'll be** jobs for us to do every day.	**There's been** a tradition that the teachers all cook breakfast for us.

To show that something exists in our world we use *there + be*: *there is/was, there are/were, there has/have been, there will be, there is/are going to be*, etc.
There can be followed by a singular or plural form of the verb *be*. The choice of singular or plural depends on the noun that comes after the verb.
For questions, the form of *be* is placed before *there*.

1 Listen. Circle the correct form of *be*. 🎧 039

1. There **is / are / were** a lot of missing pieces in this chess set.
2. There **were / will be / are** too many people at the festival.
3. Did you say there **will be / was / is** a traditional dance?
4. In next year's exhibition there **will be / are going to be / have been** some bones from 2,000 years ago!
5. There **have been / are / will be** giant stones here for ages!
6. Someone has moved my pieces. There **was / is / were** an empty space here before!
7. You said there **aren't / won't be / weren't** any pieces for this game, but I've found some!
8. The king's descendants are still alive. There **were / is / are** six grandchildren in India.

2 Read. Match the graph to the sentence. Write A, B, or C.

A. There was very little education for girls one hundred years ago.

B. There has been an increase in primary-school-aged girls in school.

C. In the future we hope that there will be more girls in schools.

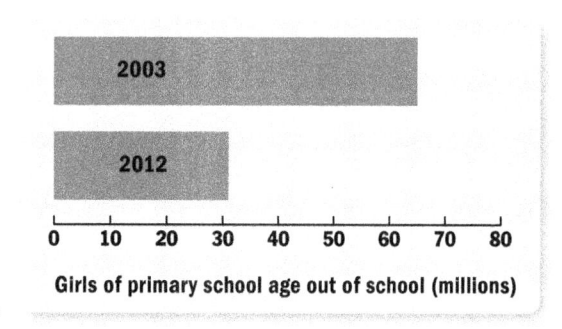

2003
2012
0 10 20 30 40 50 60 70 80
Girls of primary school age out of school (millions)

3 **Write.** Read the conversations and write *there* + the correct form of *be* in the spaces.

1. Is there a spinner for this game?

    Yes, _____there's_____ a special spinner with pictures instead of numbers.

2. Are there any ancient sites here?

    No, unfortunately _____ any ancient sites to visit.

3. Has there been any interest from the newspapers about this new site?

    There's been a little. _____ a few questions from a local magazine, but we haven't contacted all of the newspapers yet.

4 **Read and listen.** Tick **T** for *True* and **F** for *False*. 🎧040

Carrom: An ancient game

The board Carrom is a game that's played on a smooth, flat, wooden board. In each corner there's a circular hole about 2 in. (5 cm.) in diameter, and underneath each hole there's a net pocket to catch the pieces.

The pieces Each player has a 'striker' piece about 2 in. in diameter. There are also nine dark pieces and nine light pieces, plus a red piece called the 'Queen'. People often have their own strikers, which are sometimes made of bone and so are heavier than the wooden pieces.

Preparation The Queen is placed in the centre of the board. Six pieces form a circle around the Queen. The remaining 12 pieces go around the first circle of six pieces.

Objective Players choose their colour and then take turns pushing their striker piece against the other pieces. The goal is to get your pieces into the corner pockets. The winner is the player who has put all his or her pieces in the pockets first. However, it's not just a simple race. Neither player wins until one player has put the Queen in a pocket, too.

	T	F
1. On a Carrom board there are round holes in each corner.	☐	☐
2. There are 20 pieces, including two strikers and the Queen.	☐	☐
3. The heaviest piece in Carrom is the striker.	☐	☐
4. Players use their strikers to push their pieces into the holes at the corners.	☐	☐
5. The game ends when there are no pieces on the board but the Queen.	☐	☐

5 **Write.** Re-read the description of Carrom. Then write a short paragraph describing a board game you know and enjoy playing.

WRITING

When you write a classification paragraph – one on festivals, for example – it's a good idea to separate it into parts, such as: *festival music, food, origins*. Start with a topic sentence to introduce your paragraph. Describe each part using different details and examples. When you finish, write a concluding sentence to connect the separate parts back to the first topic sentence.

1 Organise.

1. Your task is to describe a traditional festival or celebration from your culture. Decide on your topic. Decide how to divide your topic into two or three parts.

2. Plan your writing. Research the topic. You'll need an introductory topic sentence. Your topic sentence will describe the festival or celebration. Write your topic sentence here:

   _____

   Next, you'll need to add details for each part of your paragraph. Make a list of details for each part.

   _____

   _____

   _____

   _____

   Remember to finish your paragraph with a conclusion. Write your concluding sentence here:

   _____

   _____

2 Write.

1. Go to page 139 in your book. Re-read the model and writing prompt.
2. Write your first draft. Check for organisation, content, punctuation, capitalisation and spelling.
3. Write your final draft. Share it with your teacher and classmates.

Now I can ...

- **talk about events in the past.**

    Describe something that happened last month or last year. Write two or three sentences.

    ☐ Yes, I can!
    ☐ I think I can.
    ☐ I need more practice.

    _____
    _____
    _____

- **describe actions that started in the past and continue into the present.**

    ☐ Yes, I can!
    ☐ I think I can.
    ☐ I need more practice.

    Complete the sentences using verbs in the present perfect form.

    1. Many people from Kenya (continue) _____ winning prizes in international sports competitions.

    2. One researcher (discover) _____ that teaching chess is helpful in many areas of education.

    3. Surprisingly, when observing less advanced civilisations, we (learn) _____ more about our own culture.

- **express existence at different points of time using *there + to be*.**

    ☐ Yes, I can!
    ☐ I think I can.
    ☐ I need more practice.

    Complete the sentences with *there + to be*.

    1. We saw that _____ bones from adult skeletons at the site.

    2. I have a question: _____ any jobs to do at the education camp next week?

    3. I don't think _____ a black queen piece in this old chess set.

- **write a classification paragraph.**

    ☐ Yes, I can!
    ☐ I think I can.
    ☐ I need more practice.

    Describe a game.

    _____
    _____
    _____

YOU DECIDE Choose an activity. Go to page 96.

Units 7–8 Review

1 Read. Choose the correct word to complete the sentences.

1. I've looked up the word ____ on the Internet, and it says it's a blood relative, for example a child born to a parent, connected to older ancestors.
   a. 'advanced'   b. 'civilisation'   c. 'descendant'

2. Can you please ____ the game? I've waited five minutes for my turn already!
   a. discover   b. continue   c. believe

3. Can you believe the Wi-Fi here? I've downloaded the complete video already! It's the ____ Internet access in town!
   a. fast   b. faster   c. fastest

4. These gadgets use too much power. My ____ has died already after only an hour!
   a. microphone   b. battery   c. screen

5. My art project ____ fun. We'll design new king and queen chess pieces.
   a. is going to be   b. are going to be   c. will

6. Have you seen the smartphones with the Chinese ____ app? You can type in Chinese.
   a. find   b. camera   c. keyboard

2 Listen. Number the pictures in the order you hear them described in the radio show. Then listen again and answer the questions. 🎧 041

____   ____   ____

1. What is another name for the Chinese New Year festival?

   _____

2. Which digital Chinese New Year apps have people downloaded?

   _____

3. What have been traditional New Year gifts in the past?

   _____

88

3 Read. Decide which answer (*a*, *b* or *c*) is not true. Circle the letter.

> Dear Barbara,
>
> There's going to be a festival in our village next summer! Will you be free to visit? I've joined the festival planning group, so it'll be more exciting for teenagers. Before, only adults decided on the food and music, and there weren't any games. I've started to search the Internet for the most interesting festival games and music. Last year there was a local band. They weren't the best but they were fun. This year the music is going to be even better - I'm the DJ! Please send any helpful advice you have, and any suggestions for music downloads!
>
> Check your calendar - it's going to be incredible!
>
> Hope to see you soon,
>
> Mike

1. Mike asks his friend Barbara
   a. to visit his village festival next summer.
   b. to be a DJ at the festival.
   c. to help him choose music.

2. Last year
   a. there weren't any games.
   b. the adults chose the entertainment.
   c. there was Mexican food.

3. Mike thinks that
   a. the local band was the worst thing at the festival.
   b. DJ music will be more exciting for teenagers.
   c. the festival will be better next summer.

4. Barbara
   a. was asked to send ideas about the music.
   b. was asked to give advice to Mike.
   c. is going to be in the festival planning group.

4 Write. Re-read Mike's e-mail in Activity 3 and write a reply. Ask questions about the events last year and the events planned for this year. Use the present perfect, *will* and *going to* questions.

_____

_____

_____

YOU DECIDE Choose an activity.   Unit 5

☐ **1** Complete the quiz about fashion. Then write two more questions for your classmates.

1. Which fabric is strong, practical and blue? _____

2. When a jacket and trousers are made from the same fabric, we call it a _____ .

3. Many people wear these at school or work. _____

4. What can people wear to make them look taller? _____

☐ **2** Change the regular verbs in the box to the past simple. Then use the past simple verbs to describe fashion through history.

decorate	dress up	look
paint	pierce	protect
replace	use	

☐ **3** Change the irregular verbs in the box to the past simple. Then use the past simple verbs to describe fashion through history. Explain why people did those things.

| have | put | think | wear |

Example: *People wore headscarves because they wanted to be formal and protect their heads from the sun.*

☐ **4** **Work in pairs.** Take turns talking about clothes. Think of a piece of clothing. Describe it, but don't say its name. Can your partner guess?

Example: *It's casual. We wear it on our heads. It's good for playing sports. It's colourful. It might have the name of a sports team on it.*
Answer: *baseball cap*

Repeat the activity in class, or make a video on your phone or tablet.

☐ **5** **Write.** Choose some clothes you like. Describe them.

- To plan your writing, follow the steps on page 54 in your workbook.
- Illustrate and display your work for your classmates to read.

☐ **6** Your teacher asks you to design clothes for a drama project.

Dramatic Clothing

- Think about a film character or a character from history, for example, Superman or Queen Elizabeth I.
- Describe his or her clothes. Remember to describe head gear, shoes, jewellery and accessories.

Describe your ideas for your character's clothes. Write at least 100 words.

YOU DECIDE Choose an activity.   Unit 6

☐ **❶** Talk about the 21st-century music business. Use words from the list.

combine	download	edit
fan	hit	hybrid
imagine	imitate	mix
opinion	perform	record
song	version	video

☐ **❷** Compare the pairs.

electronic music / traditional music

a live performance / an audio recording

CDs / downloads

original recording / cover version (copy)

Example: *I prefer original songs, not copies of the original. Original songs are simpler.*

☐ **❸** Grandma calls you from the supermarket. Answer her questions about the shopping list. Use countable and uncountable nouns.

> Hello dear!
> Sorry, I forgot my shopping list. Please help. Is there some tomato sauce in the fridge? How much is there? Are there any biscuits in the cupboard? Do I need butter? Coffee? Bread? Sugar?

☐ **❹** **Work in pairs.** You want to make something completely new. Discuss ideas with a partner. Role-play the dialogue.

- Choose two things to mix together.
- Think about sports and games, music, animals, food, art or fashion. Make a mash-up! What did you mash up? What is your new invention called?
- Practise the dialogue.
- Act out the dialogue in class, or use a phone or tablet to make a video.

☐ **❺** **Write.** Use examples and details to describe a mash-up sport, food, type of fashion, music or art.

- To plan your writing, follow the steps on page 64 of your workbook.
- Show your writing to your teacher and classmates.

☐ **❻** **Write.** Your teacher asks you to write about an example of a mash-up. This is the title you will use:

> 1 + 1 = 3?
> My mash-up!

Write at least 100 words.

95

YOU DECIDE Choose an activity.   Units 7–8

☐ **1 Work in pairs.** Put the words in the box in order from 1 to 5. (1 = the coolest and 5 = the least cool.) Explain your choices to a partner.

| a computer game | a sports gadget | a music app |
| a tablet | a smartphone | |

Now put the things in order of practicality, from the most to the least practical. Explain your thinking.

☐ **2** List several activities you plan to do next week. Are you going to do anything practical or interesting? Or maybe something incredible?

practical	interesting	incredible

☐ **3 Write.** Choose a product that has positive and negative points. Describe its good and bad points, and then give your opinion.
- To plan your writing, follow the steps on page 76 of your workbook.
- Share your writing with your teacher and classmates.

☐ **4 Write.** Below is part of a letter from an English-speaking friend.

When I come to visit you, I want to buy something from your country. Maybe you can help me think of an idea. I want something interesting and unusual. It doesn't have to be perfect! If you think of anything, please tell me about the good and bad points. Then I can choose the best thing to buy.

Respond to the letter. Write at least 100 words.

☐ **1** How have archaeologists helped us learn about our world? Use words from the list. Make sentences using present perfect verbs.

Example: *They have discovered bones under the sea.*

advanced	ancestors	bones	civilisation
descendant	origins	site	skeleton
skull	species		

☐ **2 Work in pairs.** Choose a word from Activity 1. Have a conversation about it using *there + be*. Repeat the activity in class, or make a video on a phone or tablet.

☐ **3 Write.** Choose a game that you enjoy playing. Describe it in detail. Classify the different parts of the game.
- To plan your writing, follow the steps on page 86 in your workbook.
- Share your writing with your teacher and classmates.

☐ **4** Below is part of an e-mail you received from an Australian friend.

Hello,
I'm writing a blog about Internet games for teenagers. Do you know any cool games? I'm thinking about games related to education or culture. I'm also interested in games that help with maths, or maybe language learning. I DON'T want to write about games that involve racing or fighting. Can you please help me by explaining your favourite educational Internet game?

Write a reply. Write at least 100 words.